T0198951

An Analysis of

Elizabeth F. Loftus's

Eyewitness Testimony

William J. Jenkins

Published by Macat International Ltd
24:13 Coda Centre, 189 Munster Road, London SW6 6AW.

Distributed exclusively by Routledge
2 Park Square, Milton Park, Abingdon, Oxon OX14 4RN
711 Third Avenue, New York, NY 10017, USA

Routledge is an imprint of the Taylor & Francis Group, an informa business

www.macat.com
info@macat.com

Cataloguing in Publication Data
A catalogue record for this book is available from the British Library.
Library of Congress Cataloguing-in-Publication Data is available upon request.
Cover illustration: Etienne Gilfillan

ISBN 978-1-912303-62-5 (hardback)
ISBN 978-1-912128-78-5 (paperback)
ISBN 978-1-912282-50-0 (e-book)

Notice
The information in this book is designed to orientate readers of the work under analysis,
to elucidate and contextualise its key ideas and themes, and to aid in the development
of critical thinking skills. It is not meant to be used, nor should it be used, as a
substitute for original thinking or in place of original writing or research. References and
notes are provided for informational purposes and their presence does not constitute
endorsement of the information or opinions therein. This book is presented solely for
educational purposes. It is sold on the understanding that the publisher is not engaged
to provide any scholarly advice. The publisher has made every effort to ensure that
this book is accurate and up-to-date, but makes no warranties or representations with
regard to the completeness or reliability of the information it contains. The information
and the opinions provided herein are not guaranteed or warranted to produce particular
results and may not be suitable for students of every ability. The publisher shall not be
liable for any loss, damage or disruption arising from any errors or omissions, or from
the use of this book, including, but not limited to, special, incidental, consequential or
other damages caused, or alleged to have been caused, directly or indirectly, by the
information contained within.

CONTENTS

THE MACAT LIBRARY

The Macat Library is a series of unique academic explorations of seminal works in the humanities and social sciences – books and papers that have had a significant and widely recognised impact on their disciplines. It has been created to serve as much more than just a summary of what lies between the covers of a great book. It illuminates and explores the influences on, ideas of, and impact of that book. Our goal is to offer a learning resource that encourages critical thinking and fosters a better, deeper understanding of important ideas.

Each publication is divided into three Sections: Influences, Ideas, and Impact. Each Section has four Modules. These explore every important facet of the work, and the responses to it.

This Section-Module structure makes a Macat Library book easy to use, but it has another important feature. Because each Macat book is written to the same format, it is possible (and encouraged!) to cross-reference multiple Macat books along the same lines of inquiry or research. This allows the reader to open up interesting interdisciplinary pathways.

To further aid your reading, lists of glossary terms and people mentioned are included at the end of this book (these are indicated by an asterisk [*] throughout) – as well as a list of works cited.

Macat has worked with the University of Cambridge to identify the elements of critical thinking and understand the ways in which six different skills combine to enable effective thinking.
Three allow us to fully understand a problem; three more give us the tools to solve it. Together, these six skills make up the **PACIER** model of critical thinking. They are:

ANALYSIS – understanding how an argument is built
EVALUATION – exploring the strengths and weaknesses of an argument
INTERPRETATION – understanding issues of meaning

CREATIVE THINKING – coming up with new ideas and fresh connections
PROBLEM-SOLVING – producing strong solutions
REASONING – creating strong arguments

To find out more, visit **WWW.MACAT.COM.**

CRITICAL THINKING AND *EYEWITNESS TESTIMONY*

Primary critical thinking skill: INTERPRETATION
Secondary critical thinking skill: CREATIVE THINKING

Understanding evidence is critical in a court of law – and it is just as important for critical thinking.

Elizabeth Loftus, a pioneering psychologist, made a landmark contribution to both these areas in *Eyewitness Testimony*, a trail-blazing work that undermines much of the decision-making made by judges and juries by pointing out how flawed eyewitness testimony actually is. Reporting the results of an eye-opening series of experiments and trials, Loftus explores the ways in which – unbeknownst to the witnesses themselves – memory can be distorted and become highly unreliable.

Much of Loftus's work is based on expert use of the critical thinking skill of interpretation. Her work not only highlights multiple problems of definition with regard to courtroom testimony, but also focuses throughout on how best we can understand the meaning of the available evidence. *Eyewitness Testimony* is arguably the best place in the Macat library to begin any investigation of how to use and understand interpretation.

ABOUT THE AUTHOR OF THE ORIGINAL WORK

Elizabeth F. Loftus was born in Los Angeles, California, in 1944. While at graduate school at Stanford University, she began to focus on the ways in which human memory works. After receiving her PhD, Loftus taught at the University of Washington and began looking at how memory affected American society—and the criminal justice system in particular. Her work led to crucial reforms in how eyewitness testimony is gathered and used in court.

During her career, Loftus has published many articles and has won a number of prestigious awards. She is now seen as one of the most influential figures in modern psychology.

ABOUT THE AUTHOR OF THE ANALYSIS

Dr Bill Jenkins holds a PhD in psychology from the University of Michigan. He is currently co-chair of the Department of Psychology at Mercer University.

ABOUT MACAT

GREAT WORKS FOR CRITICAL THINKING

Macat is focused on making the ideas of the world's great thinkers accessible and comprehensible to everybody, everywhere, in ways that promote the development of enhanced critical thinking skills.

It works with leading academics from the world's top universities to produce new analyses that focus on the ideas and the impact of the most influential works ever written across a wide variety of academic disciplines. Each of the works that sit at the heart of its growing library is an enduring example of great thinking. But by setting them in context – and looking at the influences that shaped their authors, as well as the responses they provoked – Macat encourages readers to look at these classics and game-changers with fresh eyes. Readers learn to think, engage and challenge their ideas, rather than simply accepting them.

'Macat offers an amazing first-of-its-kind tool for interdisciplinary learning and research. Its focus on works that transformed their disciplines and its rigorous approach, drawing on the world's leading experts and educational institutions, opens up a world-class education to anyone.'

Andreas Schleicher
Director for Education and Skills, Organisation for Economic
Co-operation and Development

'Macat is taking on some of the major challenges in university education ... They have drawn together a strong team of active academics who are producing teaching materials that are novel in the breadth of their approach.'

Prof Lord Broers,
former Vice-Chancellor of the University of Cambridge

'The Macat vision is exceptionally exciting. It focuses upon new modes of learning which analyse and explain seminal texts which have profoundly influenced world thinking and so social and economic development. It promotes the kind of critical thinking which is essential for any society and economy.
This is the learning of the future.'

Rt Hon Charles Clarke, former UK Secretary of State for Education

'The Macat analyses provide immediate access to the critical conversation surrounding the books that have shaped their respective discipline, which will make them an invaluable resource to all of those, students and teachers, working in the field.'

Professor William Tronzo, University of California at San Diego

WAYS IN TO THE TEXT

KEY POINTS

- Elizabeth F. Loftus (b. 1944) is an American psychologist who studies memory; psychology* is the study of the human mind and behavior.
- Loftus's book *Eyewitness Testimony* explains that since human memory is imperfect, eyewitness testimony* (a person's account of something they have observed) can be unreliable; on this basis, she argues for major changes to the American criminal justice system* (the system of organizations that enforces the law and prosecutes criminals).
- *Eyewitness Testimony* is important because it uses psychological research to make informed recommendations for the criminal justice system.

Who Is Elizabeth F. Loftus?

Elizabeth F. Loftus, the author of *Eyewitness Testimony* (1979), is an American psychologist who studies human memory. She earned a bachelor's degree in psychology and mathematics from the University of California at Los Angeles in 1966, and went on to receive a master's degree and a PhD from Stanford University.

After finishing at Stanford in 1970, Loftus took a job at the New School for Social Research in New York City. In 1973, she accepted a position at the University of Washington, where she remained until 2002. Today, Loftus is a distinguished professor in several academic departments at the University of California, Irvine, and an affiliate professor of psychology and law* at the University of Washington.

Loftus has had a distinguished career as a scientist, receiving many honors and awards during her career, and publishing 19 books and countless academic articles. Of these, *Eyewitness Testimony* won the National Media Award for Distinguished Contribution from the American Psychological Foundation in 1980.

Loftus was elected to both the National Academy of Sciences in Washington, DC in 2004 and the Royal Society of Edinburgh in Scotland in 2005. She served as the president of the American Psychological Association* (the foremost professional organization in the US for those who study psychology), was named the president of the American Psychology-Law Society, and won the prestigious Grawemeyer Prize in Psychology in 2005. She was named the 58th most eminent psychologist and the most influential female psychologist of the twentieth century in the *Review of General Psychology* in 2002.

What Does *Eyewitness Testimony* Say?

Loftus's purpose in *Eyewitness Testimony* is to encourage reforms in the American criminal justice system. She had noticed that many innocent people were being convicted, and that these convictions were often the result of eyewitness testimony.

Loftus begins the book by describing how important eyewitness testimony is to the criminal justice system. She also cites a number of cases in which convictions were wrongfully made that had been based on eyewitness accounts, and notes that juries regard eyewitness testimonies as particularly convincing evidence.

Loftus points out that human memory—on which eyewitness testimony is based—is not perfect. She lays out the stages of memory, which include *acquisition*,* in which information enters the memory system; *retention*,* in which information is stored; and *retrieval*,* the recall or access of that information.

There are a number of reasons why these stages do not result in completely accurate recreations of a situation or person. For example, Loftus shows that memory can be affected by stress and by information discovered after the memory was acquired. Loftus also demonstrates that retrieval can be affected by such factors as the way a question about the memory is phrased (which is called linguistic framing),* and the physical surroundings in which memory retrieval occurs.

Consequently, Loftus argues, we should recognize that neither memory nor eyewitness testimony is perfect. She calls for changes in how police ask questions in order to limit the factors that distort memory, supports new methods for how eyewitnesses identify suspects in police lineups, and advocates that psychologists should provide expert testimony about eyewitness accounts in criminal proceedings. She even provides a transcript of an expert's testimony to show what kinds of information expert witnesses can provide.

Her arguments ultimately led to substantial changes in how the criminal justice system operated in the US. For example, there are now standard procedures for collecting eyewitness testimony and for how witnesses should identify suspects.

The book also led to an increase in the number of psychologists who were called on to provide expert testimony in criminal trials. In fact, since publishing *Eyewitness Testimony,* Loftus herself has offered expert testimony in many criminal trials.

Finally, Loftus's work modeled how researchers could apply their findings to real-world settings. Her work has been critical to the development of a new academic field, psychology and law, which focuses on how psychological principles can be used to inform legal proceedings.

Why Does *Eyewitness Testimony* Matter?

Loftus's ideas, in contradicting many widely held assumptions, should interest anybody who studies memory. Readers of the book will gain a sophisticated understanding of how our memories work. One of Loftus's core ideas is that memory is imperfect, and she demonstrates this in a number of ways; she describes, for example, situations in which eyewitnesses seem uncertain about a particular event when interviewed immediately following that event, but report much higher confidence when they later testify in a legal setting.

Eyewitness Testimony is appealing for anybody who studies psychology, as it provides insight into empirical research* (research based on data gathered from direct observation) and scientific reasoning. It is, what is more, historically important: Loftus's work has changed psychology as an academic discipline by showing how psychologists' research interests are relevant outside the academic field.

Lastly, *Eyewitness Testimony* is an important text for anyone interested in learning about the overlap between psychology and the criminal justice system. In using psychological findings to argue for changes to the ways in which eyewitness testimony is gathered and used, the book proves that psychological research can improve the legal system. Loftus's commitment to this work shows the value of publically funded research.

THE AUTHOR AND THE HISTORICAL CONTEXT

KEY POINTS

- *Eyewitness Testimony* offers insights into the unreliable nature of memory—and therefore, the unreliable nature of eyewitness testimony* (accounts of events given by those who claim have seen them).

- Loftus's time at the New School for Social Research in New York City convinced her to look for ways in which her research could improve social institutions (such as the criminal justice system*—the institutions such as the police and the courts that exist to enforce laws and prosecute those who break them).

- After joining the faculty at the University of Washington in 1973, Loftus began to collaborate with the chief trial attorney in the Seattle public defender's office; this helped her become the first expert witness on eyewitness testimony in the state of Washington.

Why Read This Text?

Elizabeth F. Loftus's *Eyewitness Testimony* was originally published in 1979 and a second edition appeared in 1996. The book was written to challenge existing assumptions that eyewitness testimony was reliable and accurate. While the text draws on principles that had long been accepted in psychology,* the book was innovative in how it applied these principles to a real-world context: the criminal justice system.

Loftus believed that because her research was funded by the

> **❝** A major reason for my writing this book has been a long-standing concern with cases in which an innocent person has been falsely identified, convicted, and even jailed. **❞**
>
> Elizabeth F. Loftus, *Eyewitness Testimony*

government, it was her responsibility to improve the way in which the government-operated criminal justice system worked. She was concerned with how often forensic science* (the use of scientific methods and knowledge to solve crimes) was subsequently able to prove that people had been wrongly incarcerated (and in some cases executed). The reason for this, she believed, was that eyewitness testimony was overvalued. As she put it, "eyewitness testimony is among the most damning of all evidence that can be used in a court of law," and once it was used, "the case is as good as over."[1]

Loftus argues that eyewitness testimony can be unreliable and inaccurate. To support this claim, she describes how memory works, presenting data from a number of studies that call into question how accurately a person can precisely recreate what they have observed. She suggests that we should see memory as "highly malleable* and subject to change and distortion."[2] Loftus believed her text was important for "lawyers, psychologists, and students" because it could help them to understand "the behavior of the eyewitnesses to crimes, accidents and other important events."[3]

Author's Life

Elizabeth F. Loftus was born in Los Angeles, California in 1944. She received her bachelor's degree in psychology and mathematics from the University of California, Los Angeles in 1966. She then completed her graduate studies at Stanford University, receiving her master's in psychology in 1967, and her PhD in psychology in 1970.[4]

15

Loftus went on to accept a job on the faculty at the New School for Social Research in New York City. In 1973, she became an assistant professor of psychology at the University of Washington, and in 1984 was also appointed as an adjunct professor of law. Loftus is currently serving as distinguished professor of multiple academic departments and programs at the University of California, Irvine, and as an affiliate professor of psychology and law* at the University of Washington.[5]

Over the course of her career, Loftus has received numerous prestigious honors and awards: in 1996, she received the American Association of Applied and Preventive Psychology's Award for Distinguished Contribution to Basic and Applied Scientific Psychology; in 2001, she received the William James Fellow Award from the Association of Psychological Science; she has been elected to both the National Academy of Sciences (2004) and the Royal Society of Edinburgh (2005); in 2005, she was awarded the Grawemeyer Prize in Psychology (which carried with it a monetary prize of $200,000). She was named the 58th most eminent psychologist of the twentieth century in the *Review of General Psychology* in 2002, and she has been awarded six different honorary doctorate degrees since 1984.[6]

Author's Background

As an undergraduate, Loftus imagined that she would become a math teacher "because math was one thing my father and I could talk about."[7] But her career took a different direction when she became interested in psychology.

In graduate school at Stanford, she studied how information was classified and stored in memory. During this time, her work was mostly theoretical*— she did not focus, that is, on how her research might be used in a real-world setting. After becoming an assistant professor at the New School of Social Research, she realized, however, that she wanted her research to be socially relevant.

With this in mind, she began to adapt her research agenda toward work that would affect the world beyond the academic setting,[8] beginning (for example) to integrate her expertise on memory and her interest in crime and the criminal justice system. Then, in 1973, while working as an assistant professor at the University of Washington, Loftus began to collaborate with the chief trial attorney at the Seattle public defender's office. This experience led her to recognize how her research might affect and improve the criminal justice system.

The 1970s were a time of significant social upheaval in the United States. In response to civil unrest, the criminal justice system had been expanded, and sentences had become harsher.[9] Loftus's work was especially important in this context, as she became the first expert witness to provide testimony about how eyewitness accounts could be inaccurate or unreliable. Since then, she has served as an expert witness in a number of high-profile criminal cases.

NOTES

1   Elizabeth F. Loftus, *Eyewitness Testimony* (Cambridge, MA: Harvard University Press, 1996), v.

2   Loftus, *Eyewitness Testimony*, xiii.

3   Loftus, *Eyewitness Testimony,* vi.

4   *Famous Psychologists*, "Elizabeth Loftus," accessed December 1, 2015, http://www.famouspsychologists.org/elizabeth-loftus/.

5   University of California Irvine School of Social Ecology, "Elizabeth F. Loftus: Curriculum Vitae," http://socialecology.uci.edu/faculty/eloftus, accessed December 1, 2015.

6   Steven J. Haggbloom et al., "The 100 Most Eminent Psychologists of the 20th Century," *Review of General Psychology* 6, no. 2 (2002): 139–52.

7   Jill Neimark, "The Diva of Disclosure, Memory Researcher Elizabeth Loftus," *Psychology Today* 29, no. 1 (January 1996): 48.

8   Neimark, "The Diva of Disclosure," 48.

9   Jonathan Simon, *Governing through Crime: How the War on Crime Transformed American Democracy and Created a Culture of Fear* (Oxford: Oxford University Press, 2007).

MODULE 2
ACADEMIC CONTEXT

KEY POINTS

- Memory is a major area of interest for cognitive scientists* (scholars of how the mind works).

- While trained in the theory and methods of cognitive science, Loftus wanted her work to affect real-world settings beyond academia.

- Although cognitive scientists had long been familiar with the ideas about memory that Loftus described in *Eyewitness Testimony*, nobody had previously tried to apply them to the criminal justice system.*

The Work in its Context

To write *Eyewitness Testimony* (1979), Elizabeth F. Loftus drew on ideas from cognitive science. Researchers from a range of fields including anthropology* (the study of humankind, commonly conducted through research into cultures, beliefs, and so on), computer science, linguistics* (the study of the nature and structures of language), neuroscience* (the study of the functioning of the brain and nervous system), philosophy, and psychology* (the study of the human mind and behavior), have all contributed to the field of cognitive science and what it knows about the mind.

The mind is difficult to study scientifically. It works, after all, subjectively—each person has his or her own unique rich mental experience of the world. Additionally, during the early twentieth century, psychology was dominated by the behaviorist* perspective, which held that only observable behaviors could be

> ❝ There is now a substantial body of research that bears directly on the perception, memory, and recall of complex events of the kind involved in eyewitness testimony. ❞
>
> Elizabeth F. Loftus, *Eyewitness Testimony*

studied rather than the mind, as the workings of the mind couldn't be observed.

During the 1950s, however, an intellectual movement that we now call the cognitive revolution* changed this view. During this time, cognitive science—a field drawing on the knowledge and methods of diverse other disciplines—was established.[1] Some researchers tried to understand how people developed language; others tried to create artificially intelligent computers, or turned their attention to learning and memory.

The study of memory became the primary emphasis of cognitive science. In *Eyewitness Testimony*, Loftus draws on what cognitive scientists have learned to support her argument. In her words, she offers "a theoretical framework that views eyewitness testimony* in terms of a three-stage process."[2] This three-stage process is made up of acquisition* (in which information enters the memory system), retention* (the storage of that information), and retrieval* (recall of that information).

Overview of the Field

The study of memory began before cognitive science was officially established; in *Eyewitness Testimony,* Loftus cites the famous work of Hermann Ebbinghaus,* a German psychologist who was one of the first to study memory systematically. Ebbinghaus is best known for what he called the forgetting curve,* a concept that describes, in Loftus's words, "that we forget [the details of an event] very rapidly immediately after an event, but that forgetting becomes more and more gradual as time passes."[3] Subsequent research has supported Ebbinghaus's findings.

By the time the first edition of *Eyewitness Testimony* appeared in 1979, cognitive scientists had proposed several theories of how memory worked. Loftus writes that these theories fell into several different camps. One group of theorists claimed that "information we gain from our environments is represented as a complex network of propositions."[4] For example, an image of a black Labrador playing with a Frisbee might be stored in memories as a series of propositions such as "the dog was black," "the dog was a Labrador," "the dog had a toy," "the toy was a Frisbee." Another group of theorists asserted that each of the senses was represented by a specific type of memory: the visual system for vision, the auditory system for hearing, and so on.[5]

Despite the different models, many scientists agreed that some degree of interpretation is involved in remembering. Importantly, "only part of this interpretation is based upon the environmental input that gave rise to it."[6] In other words, memory is not just a recording of our sensory experience. It is influenced and shaped by other memories, existing knowledge, and our reasoning ability.[7] Furthermore, something we learn after the event we witnessed can change what we remember about the event.

It would seem, therefore, that our original memory can be permanently altered by these factors. While this idea was widely accepted when Loftus published *Eyewitness Testimony*, cognitive scientists had not suggested how it should affect real-world contexts such as the criminal justice system.

Academic Influences

As a graduate student, Loftus worked closely with Patrick Suppes,* a man often considered a leader in establishing psychology as a formal science.[8] Suppes was known for his work with human memory and for designing computer programs that help students learn.[9]

Loftus also collaborated with the American psychologist Jonathan Freedman* on projects related to semantic memory* (memory in which our general knowledge is stored), and projects that tried to determine how our memory organizes, represents, and retrieves information. Loftus's work with Freedman was especially important because she was able to play a directive role in her own research. Their collaborations led to several articles on semantic memory.[10]

Once on the faculty at the New School of Social Research in New York City, Loftus continued to research semantic retrieval* (or how we recall our general knowledge of the world). During this time, Loftus had a conversation with a lawyer friend who asked her: "Why not study some really significant problems such as the reliability of eyewitnesses testifying to crimes?"[11] According to Loftus, it was this challenge that led her to think about how her work might affect real-world settings.

NOTES

1   George A. Miller, "The Cognitive Revolution: A Historical Perspective," *Trends in Cognitive Sciences* 7, no. 3 (March 2003): 141–4.

2   Elizabeth F. Loftus, *Eyewitness Testimony* (Cambridge, MA: Harvard University Press, 1996), xii.

3   Loftus, *Eyewitness Testimony*, 53.

4   Loftus, *Eyewitness Testimony,* 110.

5   Loftus, *Eyewitness Testimony,* 110–2.

6   Loftus, *Eyewitness Testimony,* 111.

7   Loftus, *Eyewitness Testimony,* 111.

8   William H. Batchelder and Kenneth Wexler, "Suppes' Work in the Foundations of Psychology," in *Patrick Suppes,* ed. Radu J. Bogdan (Dordrecht, Holland: Springer, 1979), 149–86.

9   Michael Friedman, "Patrick Suppes, Stanford Philosopher, Scientist, and Silicon Valley Entrepreneur, Dies at 92," *Stanford News,* November 25, 2014, http://news.stanford.edu/news/2014/november/patrick-suppes-obit-112514.html, accessed December 1, 2015.

10   Gordon H. Bower, "Tracking the Birth of a Star," in *Do Justice and Let the Sky Fall: Elizabeth F. Loftus and Her Contributions to Science, Law, and Academic Freedom,* ed. Maryanne Garry and Harlene Hayne (Mahwah, New Jersey: Lawrence Erlbaum Associates, 2007), 15–26.

11   Bower, "Tracking the Birth of a Star," 18.

MODULE 3
THE PROBLEM

KEY POINTS

- Loftus wanted to show that eyewitness testimony* was not always reliable.
- Eyewitness testimony tends to have an enormous influence on the decisions that juries make in the course of a trial.
- Loftus argues that it is important to educate jurors on the problems associated with eyewitness testimony.

Core Question

In her book *Eyewitness Testimony*, Elizabeth Loftus argues that eyewitness testimony itself is not always reliable. As a psychologist* and cognitive scientist* (scholar of the workings of the human mind), she was aware that the human memory system was not perfect, and she spends a considerable amount of time in the book outlining the various ways in which memory can fail. Though the common assumption may be "that information, once acquired by the memory system, is unchangeable,"[1] Loftus shows instead that memories can be distorted.

As a result, eyewitness accounts of criminal acts or accidents may include errors. This is important because it can lead to the wrong people being identified as suspects or criminals. To make matters worse, juries can be persuaded by somebody who speaks with confidence, even when that person's account is flawed in some way. This is why she believes it is important for people to be educated about the shortcomings of eyewitness testimony.

> ❝ The problem can be stated rather simply: on the one hand, eyewitness testimony is very believable and can wield considerable influence over the decisions reached by a jury; on the other hand, eyewitness testimony is not always reliable. ❞
>
> Elizabeth F. Loftus, *Eyewitness Testimony*

The Participants

While Loftus's explanation of how human memory works had long been accepted by her peers in cognitive science, its implications for eyewitness testimony had never been considered. Given the prominent role that eyewitness testimony often plays in the justice system and at criminal trials, making this connection was immensely important.[2] Furthermore, in demonstrating that her research had important consequences beyond the laboratory, she paved the way for others to think of how their own work might be applicable to real-world contexts.

Loftus argued that jurors should hear expert witnesses testify as to the reliability of eyewitness accounts. For example, it would be useful for juries to know that memories can be distorted between the time of the observed event and the time that witnesses appear in court. This was undoubtedly a surprising argument for the general public, as there was little awareness about the imperfections of memory at that time. Additionally, many judges then were uncomfortable with the perception that "science was wishing to assume the role of the jury."[3] Some even refused to allow psychologists to offer expert testimony.

The Contemporary Debate

The idea that experts should testify in court about memory was the most controversial aspect of *Eyewitness Testimony*. Loftus felt this was worthwhile because it would help judges and juries to make informed decisions.[4]

Not everyone in the criminal justice system* agreed, however. Some judges believed that jurors were already aware that eyewitness testimony could be faulty, and that no expert was needed.[5]

Loftus's research contradicted this stance; she argued that,while it would be difficult to estimate exactly how often eyewitness testimony is incorrect, it may occur frequently. Loftus herself states that "more than one thousand people are known to have been wrongfully convicted prior to 1986 and some of them were, tragically, executed."[6] It is no wonder, then, that she believed strongly in reforms to the way eyewitness testimony was gathered and used. In fact, in Washington in 1975, Loftus herself became the first expert to testify about the reliability of eyewitness testimony.

NOTES

1   Elizabeth F. Loftus, *Eyewitness Testimony* (Cambridge, MA: Harvard University Press, 1996), xiii.

2   Brian L. Cutler et al., "Juror Sensitivity to Eyewitness Identification Evidence," *Law and Human Behavior* 14, no. 2 (1990): 185–91.

3   Loftus, *Eyewitness Testimony*, 199.

4   Loftus, *Eyewitness Testimony,* 191.

5   Brian L. Cutler et al., "Juror Decision Making in Eyewitness Identification Cases," *Law and Human Behavior* 12, no. 1 (1988): 41–55.

6   Loftus, *Eyewitness Testimony*, vi.

MODULE 4
THE AUTHOR'S CONTRIBUTION

KEY POINTS

- Loftus suggested that eyewitness testimony* is less reliable than most people expect.

- Loftus's work has changed how eyewitnesses are questioned in court and has allowed more experts to testify in court as to why an eyewitness account might not be completely reliable.

- Loftus's work draws on what cognitive scientists* have learned about memory. She was among the first to apply these ideas outside the academic world.

Author's Aims

In *Eyewitness Testimony* Elizabeth F. Loftus wants to reform the way that the criminal justice system*—of which the police and courts are important components—gathers and uses eyewitness testimony. In particular, she is concerned with how police and attorneys interview eyewitnesses, since their techniques sometimes have the effect of distorting or skewing memories. She fears that such distortions might lead to misidentification and wrongful convictions, and laments that "only someone who has been accused of a crime he didn't commit can know just how devastating the experience can be."[1]

Loftus also wants the psychologists* who are experts in the shortcomings of memory to be able to testify at criminal trials. This, she believes, will counteract the tendency of juries to overestimate how accurate eyewitness accounts are.[2]

To support this point, Loftus cites a number of cases in which

> **❝ For more than 30 years, [Loftus] has walked around kicking the props out from under some of the sturdiest platforms in science, law, and academia. ❞**
> Maryanne Garry and Harlene Hayne, *Do Justice and Let the Sky Fall*

eyewitnesses present questionable evidence. She hopes that readers will find the possibility disturbing that these testimonies might have led to misidentifications and wrongful convictions. The solution, she suggests, is to allow juries "to hear expert testimony on the factors affecting the reliability of eyewitness identification."[3]

Approach

Loftus's main challenge is to bridge the gap between cognitive science theory and the day-to-day running of the criminal justice system. She writes that her book "faces inward to the field of experimental psychology ... and outward toward ... the legal system."[4] While the information itself was widely accepted by the scientific community, she needed to convince those beyond the academic field that the criminal justice system should change. Ultimately, achieving this goal was the most significant achievement of the text.

An important element of Loftus's argument is an overview of what psychologists know about memory. She cites a number of research studies, many of which she conducted. She also walks readers through the various stages of memory, from an event being witnessed to it being recalled at a later time. During this walk-through, she touches on the various ways that memory can be distorted at each step of the process. Finally, she describes how police and attorneys gather information from eyewitnesses. This allows her to explain how some of these techniques can reshape memories.

Contribution in Context

Much of the research that Loftus cites in *Eyewitness Testimony* was performed in her laboratory. That Loftus had already been conducting research into issues related to the fallibility* (that is, having the capability to make mistakes) of memory for events in the real world suggests that she was thinking about the issues with the criminal justice system before the book was published. She supplements her own work with that of other scientists, and with discussions of legal cases that demonstrate how an unreliable eyewitness account can affect a decision—for example, when a defendant's conviction was based solely on eyewitness testimony, despite no other evidence and a reliable alibi.

Loftus's close association and collaboration with attorneys provided additional insight into how police officers and lawyers collect information from eyewitnesses. Some of these information-gathering techniques seem to challenge the integrity of the criminal justice system by making misidentification and wrongful conviction more likely. For instance, many lineups were deemed to be biased, or the use of photo lineups followed by live lineups made the positive identification of anyone who appeared in both more likely, irrespective of their guilt. This is why Loftus feels the need to move "her laboratory results back out to the real world in her lecturing and writings for lawyers and judges and her testimony in court cases."[5]

NOTES

1   Elizabeth F. Loftus, *Eyewitness Testimony* (Cambridge, MA: Harvard University Press, 1996), vi.

2   John C. Brigham and Robert K. Bothwell, "The Ability of Prospective Jurors to Estimate the Accuracy of Eyewitness Identifications," *Law and Human Behavior* 7, no. 1 (1983): 19–30.

3   Loftus, *Eyewitness Testimony*, 201.

4   Loftus, *Eyewitness Testimony,* XIII.

5   Gordon H. Bower, "Tracking the Birth of a Star," in *Do Justice and Let the Sky Fall: Elizabeth F. Loftus and Her Contributions to Science, Law, and Academic Freedom,* ed. Maryanne Garry and Harlene Hayne (Mahwah, New Jersey: Lawrence Erlbaum Associates, 2007), 15–26.

SECTION 2
IDEAS

MODULE 5
MAIN IDEAS

KEY POINTS

- In *Eyewitness Testimony*, Loftus focuses primarily on the predominant influence of eyewitness testimony* on juries, the imperfections of human memory, and the consequences of these two facts for the criminal justice system.*

- Loftus argues both for more consistency in how eyewitness testimony is gathered and for experts to testify in front of juries about how eyewitness testimony can sometimes be unreliable.

- Loftus presents a logical and clear argument as to why it is crucial to understand the factors that make for reliable eyewitness testimony—for instance, allowing witnesses to provide their own narrative account of events before asking them questions can increase the accuracy of their testimony.

Key Themes

In *Eyewitness Testimony,* Elizabeth F. Loftus wants to raise awareness that, because human memory can be unreliable, eyewitness testimony can be, too. This is important because of the persuasive power of eyewitness accounts.

Research, Loftus writes, shows that juries value eyewitness accounts more than other kinds of evidence.[1] She cites examples of cases that turned on questionable eyewitness accounts. For instance, Loftus recounts a case where a "defendant was convicted solely because he had been identified by ... witnesses, who had

> ❝ All the evidence points rather strikingly to the conclusion that there is almost nothing more convincing than a live human being who takes the stand, points a finger at the defendant, and says 'That's the one!' ❞
>
> Elizabeth F. Loftus, *Eyewitness Testimony*

seen the gunman in the bar for only a few seconds."[2]

This is important because, as already stated, research by cognitive scientists* had determined that memory—on which eyewitness accounts are based—is not perfect. Loftus writes about the need to educate judges and jurors about this issue. The danger, she writes, is that eyewitness testimony both influences juries and is sometimes unreliable; this results in wrongful convictions that happen with disturbing regularity.

In the book's final chapter, Loftus brings all of these ideas together in an extended discussion of a robbery trial. In this case, an important witness for the prosecution becomes more certain over time that he witnessed the defendant committing the crime, although his account does not mention any of the defendant's unusual characteristics, such as a unique tattoo and a deformed left hand. He also picks a different man when asked to identify voices.

We can see, then, what is at stake in *Eyewitness Testimony*: a witness can be honest about what he believes without being right, and as a consequence, people can be wrongfully convicted and sent to prison.

Exploring the Ideas

To demonstrate the power of eyewitness testimony, Loftus describes a study she conducted in which two groups of participants are asked to determine whether a hypothetical defendant is guilty or innocent. Both groups received the same information about the case with one exception: one group read that there was an eyewitness identifying the defendant as the perpetrator. She found that her participants gave "eyewitness testimony much more weight than other sorts of evidence when reaching a verdict."[3]

The idea that eyewitness testimony might be overvalued was new for those involved with the criminal justice system. For some, it was also controversial:

Loftus cites several instances where judges refused to allow experts on memory to testify at criminal trials. In one case, "the trial court refused to admit the testimony on the grounds that 'it would not be appropriate to take from the jury their own determination as to what weight or effect to give to the evidence of the eyewitness and identifying witnesses.'"[4] Unfortunately, research has indicated that jurors don't always recognize the limitations of eyewitness testimony.[5] This is especially troubling when a case hinges on such an account.

To some extent, this is still an issue today. For example, in 2011, the Supreme Court of New Jersey (the highest legal authority in the US state of New Jersey) issued a ruling including the assertion that eyewitness testimony is "the single greatest cause of wrongful convictions."[6]

Of course, the reason eyewitness testimony can be unreliable is that memory itself is often unreliable. For example, Loftus notes that stress can have profound effects on a person's memory, and people who experience high stress "concentrate more and more on [only] a few features of their environment, paying less and less attention to others."[7] That is, the more stress people experience, the less accurately they remember an event. We can imagine that witnessing a crime is quite stressful, and that witnesses are therefore likely to experience stress during the crucial moments when a crime is being committed.

Furthermore, Loftus shows that the longer the time between observing an event and testifying about it, the more skewed memories can become. In fact, Loftus's analysis leaves readers wondering whether or not memory can ever be considered an objective representation of what somebody actually saw.

She draws from both legal scholars and research in cognitive psychology* to make her case. Legal scholars knew that eyewitness testimony was often central to the outcomes of criminal proceedings, but they did not formally recognize that it wasn't always accurate. Cognitive scientists, on the other hand, knew that memory was not accurate, but they had never asked what the consequences of this understanding were for the criminal justice system. By combining their perspectives, Loftus makes a compelling argument for changing how eyewitness testimony is gathered, and for the need for experts to educate judges and jurors about the shortcomings of eyewitness testimony.

Language and Expression

Loftus is said to have "an engaging, informal style of conveying her findings... using easily accessible ideas characterized by catchy phrases,"[8] and she does indeed explain her points in simple, clear language. She is masterful in explaining complex research so that readers can understand how it was conducted and what its implications are. By consistently returning to key studies, she maintains her argument's integrity.

Her writing is also lively and engaging; the real-world examples help to explain the scientific concepts so that they are easily understood. The text is well organized and each chapter builds upon the one before it. The book culminates in the description of a real criminal case that illustrates why cognitive scientific theory can improve the criminal justice system. In short, Loftus succeeds in making *Eyewitness Testimony* accessible and interesting to a general audience.

NOTES

1   Elizabeth F. Loftus, *Eyewitness Testimony* (Cambridge, MA: Harvard University Press, 1996), 10.

2   Loftus, *Eyewitness Testimony*, xi.

3   Loftus, *Eyewitness Testimony,* 10.

4   Loftus, *Eyewitness Testimony,* 194.

5   John C. Brigham and Robert K. Bothwell, "The Ability of Prospective Jurors to Estimate the Accuracy of Eyewitness Identifications," *Law and Human Behavior* 7, no. 1 (1983): 19–30.

6   Findlaw, "State v. Henderson," Supreme Court of New Jersey (August 24, 2011), http://caselaw.findlaw.com/nj-supreme-court/1578475.html, accessed February 16, 2016.

7   Loftus, *Eyewitness Testimony*, 35.

8   Gordon H. Bower, "Tracking the Birth of a Star," in *Do Justice and Let the Sky Fall: Elizabeth F. Loftus and Her Contributions to Science, Law, and Academic Freedom,* ed. Maryanne Garry and Harlene Hayne (Mahwah, New Jersey: Lawrence Erlbaum Associates, 2007), 15–26.

MODULE 6
SECONDARY IDEAS

KEY POINTS

- In addition to the main argument, Loftus describes how human memory and the criminal justice system* work in general.

- These secondary ideas form a foundation for Loftus's argument about what reforms would benefit the criminal justice system.

- Her claims ultimately resulted in changes to how eyewitnesses were used in criminal proceedings, and she also encouraged other psychologists* to consider how their research could affect society.

Other Ideas

In order to support her main argument in *Eyewitness Testimony*, Elizabeth F. Loftus provides an overview of how human memory works. She writes that our memory system consists of three parts: acquisition,* retention,* and retrieval.* Acquisition refers to the point at which we take in information; retention describes the stage when we store or organize that information; and retrieval is when we recall it at a later time. This overview is more than just a survey of cognitive science's* theories of memory, however; Loftus also shows how these systems work in real-world scenarios.

Loftus is particularly interested in "the effects of events that occur while the to-be-remembered information is resident in the memory system."[1] In other words, she wants to know the consequences of things that happen to us between the time that we witness an event and the time that we describe it from our memories. Her research

> ❝ When we experience an important event, we do not simply record that event in memory as a videotape recorder would. ❞
>
> Elizabeth F. Loftus, *Eyewitness Testimony*

seems to indicate that what happens to us in this in-between time might affect the way we remember.

She also points out that the way questions are phrased can affect memories. Accordingly, the way in which witnesses are asked to identify criminals can, unfortunately, affect the way that those witnesses answer.

Exploring the Ideas

Loftus wanted readers to understand that memories could be influenced and reshaped at each of the three stages of the memory system (acquisition, retention, and retrieval).

In order to remember something, we must, of course, first perceive it. However, Loftus notes that even in situations in which "an event is bright, loud enough, and close enough, and even though attention is being paid, we can still find significant errors in a witnesses recollection of the event, and it is common for two witnesses to the same event to recall it very differently."[2]

In other words, even when we closely observe a phenomenon, a range of factors can affect how we remember it. Some of these factors include how long we spend witnessing the event, the number of opportunities we have to observe it, and how striking specific details are to us. Additionally, witnesses are affected by how stressed they are, what they expect to happen, and any personal biases—even unconscious ones—they might have.

Once we have acquired a memory, a new set of problems arises that can prevent us from accurately describing what we witnessed.

One problem at this stage that Loftus is particularly concerned with is linguistic framing*—the idea that the way an interviewer phrases questions to an eyewitness can shape that eyewitness's answer.

For example, in one study, Loftus showed two groups of participants a recording of a traffic accident. She then asked each group slightly different versions of the same questions. Group A, for instance, was asked to estimate the speed of the cars when "they *smashed* into" each other, while group B was to estimate the speed of the cars when "they *hit* each other."

She found that group A (the "smash" group) estimated that the cars impacted at higher speeds than group B (the "hit" group). She also found that group A participants were more likely to report seeing broken glass than group B, although there was no broken glass in the video. This shows how the use of specific words can influence what witnesses think that they observed—and can inadvertently create inaccurate reports.[3]

Similarly, Loftus is able to draw on research dating back more than a century to show that the context in which a memory is recalled can shape the memory itself. That is, factors like the setting, the people in the setting, and the witness's state of mind, might play a role in what witnesses say. Loftus argues that retrieval is most accurate when it happens in a context similar to that in which the memory was originally acquired.[4] In some cases, witnesses are taken back to the scene where the crime occurred.

In addition, there are different ways in which witnesses can be asked to retrieve memories, and this can make a difference. For instance, asking a witness to recall what they observed (often called a "free-narrative report") results in an account that is more accurate, but less detailed, than a report prompted by specific questions about the details of an event.

At each turn, Loftus indicates how the information presented throughout the book has significant implications for eyewitness testimony.* This is a very effective approach as it helps readers understand that the human memory system is fallible* (capable of making mistakes). It allows the reader to understand how "a witness can get a poor glimpse, have little confidence in his future ability to make an accurate identification, and yet ultimately make a positive identification."[5]

Overlooked

While *Eyewitness Testimony* is largely remembered for showing what can go wrong in the process of acquiring, retaining, and retrieving memories, other ideas in the book merit additional attention.

It is interesting, for example, that eyewitness testimony can often be more convincing to a jury than other kinds of evidence, such as DNA profiling. Loftus's work shows that historically, verdicts have often been based on eyewitness testimony alone.

Another point of interest is how Loftus challenges assumptions about how much juries know about the way memory works. While some courts refused expert testimony on the grounds that juries understood the limitations of eyewitness account, Loftus shows that this is not necessarily the case.

NOTES

1 Elizabeth F. Loftus, *Eyewitness Testimony* (Cambridge, MA: Harvard University Press, 1996), XII.

2 Loftus, *Eyewitness Testimony,* 22.

3 Loftus, *Eyewitness Testimony,* 77–8.

4 Loftus, *Eyewitness Testimony,* 89–90.

5 Loftus, *Eyewitness Testimony,* 6.

MODULE 7
ACHIEVEMENT

KEY POINTS

- Loftus has achieved many of her goals in *Eyewitness Testimony.*

- Because she is able to write clearly and for a general audience, people from many different backgrounds and interests have been able to appreciate the importance of her argument.

- While Loftus focuses specifically on the criminal justice system,* the issues discussed in the book are also relevant to other contexts.

Assessing the Argument

Writing *Eyewitness Testimony*, Elizabeth F. Loftus's hope was to reform the way the criminal justice system gathered and used eyewitness testimony* in criminal proceedings. More specifically, she points out how the techniques that police and lawyers use in interviewing witnesses sometimes encourage witnesses to remember an event inaccurately. She also proposed that psychologists* should be able to testify in court so that judges and juries could better interpret the evidence they heard from eyewitnesses.

Her book did in fact lead to reforms. For instance, the procedure in which suspects are identified has been standardized, and the way that eyewitnesses are interviewed has been changed: now witnesses are generally asked to provide a narrative of what they saw before they are asked the kind of detail-oriented questions that might inadvertently alter their memory of the event.

Even more significantly, psychologists are increasingly allowed

> **"**In a career spanning four decades, Loftus ... has done more than any other researcher to document the unreliability of memory in experimental settings. And she has used what she has learned to testify as an expert witness in hundreds of criminal cases.**"**
>
> Moheb Costandi, "Evidence-Based Justice: Corrupted Memory"

to educate judges and jurors about the potential problems with eyewitness testimony. In the preface of the current edition of *Eyewitness Testimony*, Loftus remarks that "today, judges in many states and federal jurisdictions permit expert testimony."[1] Notably, the 2011 Supreme Court of New Jersey's ruling mentioned in module 5 was largely based on Loftus's work. That ruling acknowledged that "jurors should be alerted to the imperfect nature of memory and the fallibility of eyewitness testimony as standard procedure."[2]

Achievement in Context

As mentioned above, *Eyewitness Testimony* has profoundly influenced the American criminal justice system. Today, witnesses are questioned in more consistent ways, and many courts welcome the expert testimony of psychologists. Another change has been that psychologists and cognitive scientists* have more reason to consider how their research might be relevant beyond the academic world, Loftus showed that such work is valuable.

Much of Loftus's success is due to how clearly and logically she presents her argument. It managed to be persuasive and engaging for cognitive scientists, criminal justice professionals, and regular citizens. Ultimately, everyone benefits from a fair and just criminal justice system. It is perhaps even more impressive that Loftus made this argument at a time when the system was making punishments harsher and more frequent.

Notably, Loftus has both written and acted in favor of reforms to eyewitness testimony. In several hundred criminal proceedings she has served as the sort of expert on eyewitness testimony that she believed was necessary, and she has also worked closely with government agencies to make this practice more common.

Limitations

It should be pointed out that not everyone has welcomed these changes. In fact, some have suggested that Loftus has "harmed victims and aided murderers and rapists"[3] by challenging the reliability and accuracy of eyewitness testimony in the courtroom.

That said, the book has resonated with professional and general audiences. That a second edition was published almost two decades after the first is evidence of how persistent this interest has been.

One of the book's most unexpected consequences is the degree to which it prompted cognitive scientists to look for ways to apply their theories to real-world situations. For example, just a few years after it was published, there was an explosion of interest in psychology and law;* this new area of study applies psychological principles to inform how our legal system works.

Since 1976, writes Loftus and the American psychologist and legal scholar John Monahan* on this growing discipline, "the American Psychology-Law Society has burgeoned to record membership levels, an American Board of Forensic Psychology was created to certify expertise in courtroom matters, and in 1981, the American Psychological Association conferred official legitimacy on the area by forming Psychology and Law as its 41st Division."[4]

NOTES

1   Elizabeth F. Loftus, *Eyewitness Testimony* (Cambridge, MA: Harvard University Press, 1996), ix.

2   Moheb Costandi, "Evidence-Based Justice: Corrupted Memory," *Nature* 500, no. 7462 (August 2013): 268–70, http://dx.doi.org/10.1038/500268a, accessed February 16, 2016.

3   Costandi, "Evidence-Based Justice."

4   John Monahan and Elizabeth F. Loftus, "The Psychology of Law," *Annual Review of Psychology* 33 (February 1982): 441–75, http://dx.doi.org/10.1146/annurev.ps.33.020182.002301, accessed February 16, 2016.

MODULE 8
PLACE IN THE AUTHOR'S WORK

KEY POINTS

- Loftus has spent her career investigating how human memory works.

- *Eyewitness Testimony* represented a shift in Loftus's goals from theoretical research* (research that seeks a conceptual understanding of its subject) to considering how it might be applied outside the academic world.

- The book affirmed Loftus as an expert on memory and eyewitness testimony.*

Positioning

Eyewitness Testimony (1979) is Elizabeth F. Loftus's fourth book. She had previously been researching problem-solving and semantic memory* (memory relating to the general knowledge each person has). In particular, she focused on "how the mind classifies and remembers information."[1] During this early stage of her career, she cowrote three books on these topics: *Learning* (1973), *Human Memory: The Processing of Information* (1976), and *Cognitive Processes* (1979).[2] In these, she and her coauthors reviewed existing research and described how these processes were understood by the scientific community.

After joining the faculty of the University of Washington, Loftus began to consider how her research might be relevant beyond academia. She shifted her focus to how the fallibility* (the unreliability) of memory might have consequences for people and social institutions (such as the criminal justice system*). The studies she published on how eyewitness accounts relied on an

> ❝Loftus has spent most of her life steadily amassing a clear and brilliant body of work showing that memory is amazingly fragile and inventive.❞
>
> Jill Neimark, "The Diva of Disclosure, Memory Researcher Elizabeth Loftus"

imperfect memory system began to attract attention and formed the foundation for her arguments in *Eyewitness Testimony*—the first book she published without coauthors.

Since *Eyewitness Testimony*, Loftus has continued to research and write about subjects relevant to our legal system. Most recently, she has begun to investigate repressed memories*—memories of traumatic events that we may not be conscious of having. This has been controversial work, and it has resulted at times in significant criticism; Loftus was sued, for example, by someone she had written about in a study on repressed memories.[3]

Integration

During her successful career as a cognitive scientist,* Loftus has contributed greatly to the ways in which we understand memory and how memory operates in the real world. Her recent research on repressed memories has only increased the influence that her work has on the criminal justice system.

The main ideas of Loftus's work on repressed memories are similar to her ideas about eyewitness testimony. She argues that "specific therapeutic procedures can lead to false autobiographical memories."[4]

She and her colleague demonstrate this in an ingenious study in which research participants are presented with four childhood events. Three of these are real, but the fourth, a description of a time in which the person was lost in a large shopping mall, is not. When asked about these memories, nearly a third of the participants report having memories of the false recollection. This leads the authors to conclude that "people can be led to believe that entire events happened to them after suggestions to those effects."[5] This was one of the first demonstrations that an entire memory can be created.

As was the case for her research on the reliability of eyewitness testimony, Loftus applied her findings in criminal proceedings. One of the most famous involved a young woman who claimed that, when she was six, she had been sexually abused by her mother, and that these memories were repressed until she was 17. Though the "case has been hailed by some as the new proof of recovery of repressed or dissociated traumatic memories, and even as proof of the reliability of recovered memories of repeated abuse,"[6] Loftus and a colleague assert that "there are reasons to doubt not only the 'supporting evidence,' but also that the sexual abuse ever happened in the first place."[7] We can see in this example both how Loftus continues to expand her research into the fallibility of the human memory, and also how controversial such work can be.

Significance

What is perhaps most significant about *Eyewitness Testimony* is the shift it represents in Loftus's research goals: she had begun to ask what real-world implications her work might have.

The book also made her a well-respected authority on the problems with memory and eyewitness testimony. This is one reason that she has become a regular fixture in courtrooms around the US, where she testifies as to how eyewitness accounts can be unreliable. In this capacity, her goal is to show judges and juries that "memories are pliable and that eyewitness accounts are far from perfect recordings of actual events."[8]

While Loftus has published countless research articles, book chapters, and books, she is still best known for *Eyewitness Testimony*. This indicates the book's importance as the most significant work by one of the world's most respected and influential cognitive scientists.

NOTES

1   Jill Neimark, "The Diva of Disclosure, Memory Researcher Elizabeth
    Loftus," *Psychology Today* 29, no. 1 (January 1996): 48.

2   Sarnoff A. Mednick et al., *Learning* (Englewood Cliffs, New Jersey:
    Prentice-Hall, 1973); Geoffrey R. Loftus and Elizabeth F. Loftus, *Human
    Memory: The Processing of Information* (Hillsdale, New Jersey: Lawrence
    Erlbaum Associates, 1976); Lyle E. Bourne et al., *Cognitive Processes*
    (Englewood Cliffs, New Jersey: Prentice-Hall, 1979).

3   Gilbert Geis and Elizabeth F. Loftus, "Taus vs. Loftus: Determining the
    Legal Ground Rules for Scholarly Inquiry," *Journal of Forensic Psychology
    Practice* 9 (2009): 147–62, http://papers.ssrn.com/sol3/papers.
    cfm?abstract_id=1496006, accessed February 16, 2016.

4   Elizabeth F. Loftus and Deborah Davis, "Recovered Memories," *Annual
    Review of Clinical Psychology* 2 (April 2006): 469–98.

5   Elizabeth F. Loftus and Jacqueline E. Pickrell, "The Formation of False
    Memories," *Psychiatric Annals* 25, no. 12 (December 1995): 720–5.

6   Elizabeth F. Loftus and Melvin J. Guyer, "Who Abused Jane Doe? The
    Hazards of the Single Case History: Part I," *Skeptical Inquirer* 26, no. 3
    (2002): 24–32.

7   Loftus and Guyer, "Who Abused Jane Doe?" 24.

8   Moheb Costandi, "Evidence-Based Justice: Corrupted Memory,"
    Nature 500, no. 7462 (August 2013): 269–70, http://dx.doi.
    org/10.1038/500268a, accessed February 16, 2016.

THE FIRST RESPONSES

KEY POINTS

- The two main critiques of Loftus's work are that she may have defended potential criminals and that her laboratory research does not actually reflect real-world situations.

- Loftus contends that she has prevented innocent people from being wrongfully convicted, and that her work reflects how memory works.

- It is because of her empirical* methods of gathering data (that is, data gathered through her own direct observations) that she has been able to withstand criticism.

Criticism

The responses to Elizabeth F. Loftus's *Eyewitness Testimony* were generally quite positive. Academics and legal professionals alike applauded her effort to apply her research in meaningful ways. Furthermore, the book won the American Psychological Foundation's National Media Award for Distinguished Contribution in 1980, the year after publication, and it was popular enough that a second edition appeared in 1996.

Despite this, Loftus was criticized, especially by legal professionals, who may have assumed that her work made convicting those who were truly guilty more difficult.[1]

Additionally, some questioned the extent to which Loftus's research actually reflected the world beyond the laboratory. One scholar remarked that "psychologists* who routinely offer expert testimony to the courts about the problems of eyewitness testimony* demonstrate an unwarranted degree of faith in experimental psychology."[2] Others—such as the prosecutor of the robbery case

> ❝ She has been called a whore by a prosecutor in a courthouse hallway, assaulted by a passenger on an airplane shouting, 'You're that woman!', and has occasionally required surveillance by plainclothes security guards at lectures. The war over memory is one of the great and perturbing stories of our time, and Elizabeth Loftus ... stands at the highly charged center of it. ❞
>
> Jill Neimark, "The Diva of Disclosure, Memory Researcher Elizabeth Loftus"

described at the end of *Eyewitness Testimony*—argue that the stress and fear experienced by witnesses of a crime might not distort their memories as badly as Loftus's laboratory tests suggested.[3]

Responses

In responding to these critiques, Loftus conceded that her work might make it more difficult to convict true criminals on the basis of eyewitness testimony alone, but stated that she was more concerned with the devastating consequences of wrongful convictions. For example, in an interview in *Psychology Today*, she says, "I feel as if some of these accusers are willing to blow up a 747 full of people because there might be one suspected child molester on board. They don't care that they're ripping the hearts out of families by their absolute insistence that this crime must be true."[4]

Loftus anticipated the criticism that her laboratory research could not be generalized, and she addresses this in the book itself. She argues that her research had been designed to reflect real-world situations— much more than previous experiments had been.[5]

It should also be noted that both cognitive scientists* and legal scholars offered defenses of Loftus's work, and in so doing silenced the majority of her critics.

Conflict and Consensus

If most academics readily accepted the arguments made in *Eyewitness Testimony*, this was in part because of Loftus's existing reputation as a scholar and because of the sound empirical nature of her work. The book's success led to Loftus being invited to speak at law schools and colleges around the world. She also began to serve as an expert witness during criminal trials, some of which were very high profile.

Loftus's more recent research on repressed memories* (unconscious memories of traumatic experiences) and false memories* (apparent recollections of events that did not actually occur) has been far more controversial than *Eyewitness Testimony*. Within her field, it has sparked what is often called the "memory wars"*— the controversy in the 1990s between healthcare professionals about the reliability of repressed memories, a conflict that even today is not entirely decided. In a recent study, Loftus and colleagues concluded that those who researched memory were more skeptical about repressed memories than others.[6]

Loftus has provoked impassioned responses outside the academic world too. She received death threats, and was sometimes accompanied by bodyguards when she spoke in public.

NOTES

1   Moheb Costandi, "Evidence-Based Justice: Corrupted Memory," *Nature* 500, no. 7462 (August 2013): 269–70, http://dx.doi.org/10.1038/500268a, accessed February 16, 2016.

2   Robert G. Pachella, "Personal Values and the Value of Expert Testimony," *Law and Human Behavior* 10, no. 1–2 (June 1986): 145–50.

3   Elizabeth F. Loftus, *Eyewitness Testimony* (Cambridge, MA: Harvard University Press, 1996), 230–1.

4   Jill Neimark, "The Diva of Disclosure, Memory Researcher Elizabeth Loftus," *Psychology Today* 29, no. 1 (January 1996): 48.

5   Loftus, *Eyewitness Testimony*, 155.

6   Lawrence Patihis et al., "Are the 'Memory Wars' Over? A Scientist-Practitioner Gap in Beliefs about Repressed Memory," *Psychological Science* 25, no. 2 (February 2014): 519–30.

MODULE 10
THE EVOLVING DEBATE

KEY POINTS

- *Eyewitness Testimony* has significantly affected the American criminal justice system.*

- It has also inspired cognitive scientists* to continue expanding our knowledge of how memory works.

- Loftus' work has helped establish a field of academic study in which psychology* and the legal system overlap (called, appropriately, psychology and law*).

Uses and Problems

Since the publication of Elizabeth F. Loftus's *Eyewitness Testimony* in 1979, much has changed in the psychological and legal worlds. There are now clear and consistent guidelines for how police and attorneys can prompt witnesses to identify a suspect as a criminal.

One example of a change inspired by the book is the abandonment of the practice of showing pictures of suspects to an eyewitness before asking that witness to attempt to identify a suspect from an in-person lineup. This, Loftus wrote, was problematic. Her research demonstrated that the "chances of being falsely identified as one of the criminals" rose dramatically under these circumstances because seeing a photograph first would create a sense of familiarity that could be mistaken as a memory.[1] As a consequence, lineups conducted today minimize this possibility.

As has been stated, Loftus's work increased how often psychologists testified in court about the unreliability of eyewitnesses' memory. In the preface to the 1996 edition of *Eyewitness Testimony*, Loftus writes that "more than one hundred

> ❝ In both psychological and legal arenas, much has happened since the original publication of *Eyewitness Testimony.* Yet more than a decade later, the book is still being read by lawyers, psychologists, and students around the world. ❞
>
> Elizabeth F. Loftus, preface to *Eyewitness Testimony*

psychologists have testified in various cases as experts on eyewitness testimony."[2]

Loftus's work has inspired interest in how psychological research can be applied outside the academic discipline. Before *Eyewitness Testimony,* many more researchers valued theoretical research* (that is, research expanding a conceptual understanding rather than a practical application) over applied research* (the attempt to use concepts to explain how things happen or exist in the real world). However, Loftus's success has made applied research more appealing and prestigious.

Schools of Thought

The renewed interest in applied research and the overlap of Loftus's work with the legal system helped create the subdiscipline of psychology and law, which was officially recognized by the foremost professional organization for psychologists, the American Psychological Association (APA)*, in 1981.

According to the APA, "the American Psychology-Law Society promotes the contributions of psychology to the understanding of law and legal institutions, the education of psychologists in legal matters and law personnel in psychological matters, and the application of psychology in the legal system."[3] Given her importance in the founding of this field, it is not surprising that Loftus served as the president of the American Psychology-Law Society in 1985.

As a result of this new field, many psychologists today collaborate closely with legal scholars or even work at law schools. Furthermore, more psychologists receive legal training as a regular part of their education. According to the American Psychology-Law website, "a variety of training programs have been developed to meet the needs of students interested in interdisciplinary study and work."[4] This makes sense, of course, if the trend of having psychologists testify in court as experts is to continue.

In Current Scholarship

Loftus's work has influenced psychologists across the discipline. Prominent memory researchers who routinely cite her work as important to their own include the Estonian Canadian psychologist Endel Tulving,* currently emeritus professor of psychology at the University of Toronto; the Canadian psychologist Allan Paivio,* who specializes in how verbal and nonverbal information is stored in memory; the American psychologist and cognitive scientist* Edward E. Smith;* and the American psychologist and cognition specialist David Rumelhart.*

One example of important research that builds on Loftus's work is that of American psychologist Jonathan Schooler,* who is interested in verbal overshadowing*—the idea that verbal descriptions of a memory can make that memory less accurate. Schooler suggests that "verbalizing a visual memory may produce a verbally biased memory representation that can interfere with the application of the original visual memory."[5]

Schooler has also studied whether verbal overshadowing might have implications for eyewitness testimony and identification.[6] In one such study, participants watched a video of a bank robbery; immediately after the video, half of the participants were asked to describe the robber in as much detail as possible, and half were not. Surprisingly, participants who gave descriptions "were significantly less accurate at recognizing the target face" than those who had not been asked to describe the robber in detail.[7]

Two other researchers who have followed Loftus's lead in applying their research to the real world are Daniel Kahneman,* who won the Nobel Prize in economics in 2002, and his collaborator, the Israeli psychologist Amos Tversky.* Their research interests include economic decisionmaking and linguistic framing* (the ways in which the wording of a question can affect its interpretation).

NOTES

1   Elizabeth F. Loftus, *Eyewitness Testimony* (Cambridge, MA: Harvard University Press, 1996), 150.

2   Loftus, *Eyewitness Testimony,* ix–x.

3   American Psychological Association, "American Psychology-Law Society," http://www.apa.org/about/division/div41.aspx, accessed December 8, 2015.

4   American Psychological Association, "American Psychology-Law Society."

5   Jonathan W. Schooler and Tonya Y. Engstler-Schooler, "Verbal Overshadowing of Visual Memories: Some Things are Better Left Unsaid," *Cognitive Psychology* 22 (1990): 36–71.

6   Jason M. Chin and Jonathan W. Schooler, "Verbal Overshadowing and Eyewitness Identification," in *Encyclopedia of Psychology and Law*, ed. Brian L. Cutler (Thousand Oaks, California: Sage, 2007), 831–3.

7   Jonathan W. Schooler et al., "The Costs and Benefits of Verbally Rehearsing Memory for Faces," in *Basic and Applied Memory Research, Volume II,* ed. D. J. Herrmann et al., (Hillsdale, New Jersey: Erlbaum, 1996), 51–65.

MODULE 11
IMPACT AND INFLUENCE TODAY

KEY POINTS

- Today, *Eyewitness Testimony* is still relevant for teaching students about memory and for demonstrating how psychological research has real-world importance.

- While the book's ideas are now considered well-known facts in psychology,* Loftus's more recent work has been quite controversial.

- Loftus continues to rely on empirical* research to support her claims that human memory is imperfect.

Position

There's little doubt that Elizabeth F. Loftus achieves her goals in *Eyewitness Testimony*. Indeed, as one scholar has noted, her work "has been 'profoundly important' in shaping these changes."[1] As a result, the role of eyewitnesses within the criminal justice system* has been reformed, and it is now normal for experts to testify in court as to the reliability of eyewitness accounts.*

Despite being first published in 1979, the book is still assigned in psychology courses today to help students learn about memory and about how psychological research can be applied beyond the laboratory. It is also often found in law courses.

The book's second edition, published in 1996 and still in print, is evidence that it has remained popular long after it originally appeared. It has been one of the top-selling books in its category.

Interaction

While the ideas in *Eyewitness Testimony* have been accepted,

> ❝[Loftus's] research is starting to bring about lasting changes in the legal system.❞
>
> Moheb Costandi, "Evidence-Based Justice: Corrupted Memory"

Loftus's more recent work has caused some controversy. The ensuing debate within psychology, which was over how repressed memories* should be understood, has come to be known as the memory wars.*[2]

The memory wars center around whether or not people repress traumatic memories, and if these repressed memories can be recovered through "highly suggestive psychotherapy, which included guided imagination, dream interpretations, hypnosis, sodium amytal* administration, and 'bibliotherapy,' in which patients are given books to read that convey the theory of massive repression of childhood sexual abuse, all designed to excavate the allegedly recalcitrant trauma memories."[3]

The psychiatrist Bessel van der Kolk,* a proponent of using these techniques to uncover repressed memories, has said that it "is in the very nature of traumatic memory to be dissociated, and to be initially stored as sensory fragments without a coherent semantic* component" ("semantic" here refers to remembered knowledge). [4] There is, in fact, some evidence for this position. For instance, one therapist who uses these techniques claims that nearly two-thirds of his patients with recovered memories of childhood sexual abuse were "able to document at least one episode of the abuse that they had alleged in therapy."[5]

Loftus, however, was skeptical. She began studying repressed memory because of the increase in the number of allegations of "horrific satanic sexual abuse rings based largely on memories that emerged from problematic psychotherapy" during the 1980s and 1990s. [6] Because she had spent so much time studying how memories could be unreliable, she was unsure about the accuracy of the reported accounts.

Soon, she began to write about high-profile cases in which questionable therapeutic techniques seemed to lead to questionable accounts of past events. Not surprisingly, the responses she provoked were not always positive. For example, in an article in *Psychology Today*, van der Kolk commented, "I have nothing good to say about Elizabeth Loftus."[7]

The Continuing Debate

Loftus and her colleagues have based their arguments about repressed memories on research they have done on the psychotherapeutic techniques used to recover those memories. This has been important, since nobody had previously shown that memories of events that never happened could be created.

The "lost in the mall" study described earlier was one of the first demonstrations that this was possible. A number of subsequent studies have also been published demonstrating that researchers "can make people falsely believe that quite unusual or even traumatic events happened"[8] to them. For example, people have been led to believe that they were hospitalized for ear pain or were attacked by animals.[9]

The results of this research have been sufficiently influential that some have proclaimed the memory wars over.[10] A recent study suggests, however, that the psychological community is still divided on the matter.[11]

This is a conclusion that Loftus herself must be keenly aware of, given some of the responses her writing has received. She has been furiously critiqued and has even been sent death threats. For example, in an interview with *Psychology Today*, Loftus shared an anonymous letter she received from an incest survivor who told Loftus that her work was "on the same level as those who deny the existence of the extermination camps during [World War II]."[12]

NOTES

1   Moheb Costandi, "Evidence-Based Justice: Corrupted Memory,"
    Nature 500, no. 7462 (August 2013): 269–70, http://dx.doi.
    org/10.1038/500268a, accessed February 16, 2016.

2   Lawrence Patihis et al., "Are the 'Memory Wars' Over? A Scientist-
    Practitioner Gap in Beliefs about Repressed Memory," *Psychological
    Science* 25, no. 2 (February 2014): 519–30.

3   Elizabeth F. Loftus, "Dispatch from the (Un)civil Memory Wars," *Lancet*
    364 (December 2004): 20–1, http://dx.doi.org/10.1016/S0140-
    6736(04)17626-5, accessed February 16, 2016.

4   Bessel A. van der Kolk and Rita Fisler, "Dissociation and the Fragmentary
    Nature of Traumatic Memories: Overview and Exploratory Study," *Journal
    of Traumatic Stress* 8, no. 4 (1995): 505–25.

5   Jill Neimark, "The Diva of Disclosure, Memory Researcher Elizabeth
    Loftus," *Psychology Today* 29, no. 1 (January 1996): 48.

6   Julia Shaw, "Memory Mondays: 'Regression Therapy' isn't Real, but
    Hollywood Keeps the Myth Alive," *Scientific American*, November 23,
    2015, http://blogs.scientificamerican.com/mind-guest-blog/memory-
    mondays-regression-therapy-isn-t-real-but-hollywood-keeps-the-myth-alive/,
    accessed December 9, 2015.

7   Neimark, "The Diva of Disclosure," 48.

8   Loftus, "Dispatch from the (Un)civil Memory Wars," 20.

9   Loftus, "Dispatch from the (Un)civil Memory Wars," 20.

10 Loftus, "Dispatch from the (Un)civil Memory Wars," 20.

11 Patihis et al., "Are the 'Memory Wars' Over?" 519–30.

12 Neimark, "The Diva of Disclosure," 48.

MODULE 12
WHERE NEXT?

KEY POINTS

- *Eyewitness Testimony* will continue to be important for students in the field of psychology and law.*
- It will also continue to influence researchers who want to understand memory.
- The book will be remembered for the tremendous changes it effected in the United States criminal justice system,* as well as the interest it sparked in applied research.*

Potential

Elizabeth F. Loftus's *Eyewitness Testimony* (1979) has been incredibly influential for both the field of psychology* and the American criminal justice system. The book is also still important for students. It offers those who study psychology a clear, accessible understanding of the complexities of the human memory system, and those who study law can learn about the role that memory plays in eyewitness testimony.*

In her most recent work, Loftus has "moved from trying to affect single cases to pushing for broader changes in the legal system."[1] She has been working with several states in the United States to implement changes in the criminal justice system that will make wrongful convictions less likely.

It is also possible that Loftus's work could lead to reforms in the legal systems of other countries. However, one reason the book succeeded in the US was that Loftus was actively involved in the legal system she wrote about. If other countries wanted to adopt her reforms, they would have to adapt her arguments for their own systems.

❝*Eyewitness Testimony* presents the science and scholarship of earlier generations. After reading this material, one is fully prepared to enter contemporary laboratories and discover how research in this area is now conducted and what new empirical findings tell us about factors that influence accuracy of witnesses, as well as methods of improving their accuracy.❞

Elizabeth F. Loftus, preface to *Eyewitness Testimony*

Future Directions

While Loftus continues to expand what we know about memory, in considering the future implications of her work it is also important to consider the example she set as an academic.

Among cognitive scientists,* Loftus is revered for her innovative approach to research. Her research designs have allowed her to tap into the imperfections of memory. For this reason, even her earlier work—which was mostly theoretical*—has often been cited by leaders in the field.

She has also been instrumental in the establishment of psychology and law as a subfield of study—a field that has grown steadily since its formal recognition in the 1980s. This field's work will likely continue to contribute to an understanding of how psychological principles operate in the legal system.

In addition, Loftus has helped create an academic and intellectual culture in which applied research* (when academic research is used to explain or better understand how something works in a nonacademic environment) is valued. As a result, many contemporary psychologists are now exploring how their research interests might be useful outside academia. One such project resulted in a Nobel Prize in economics for the economist Daniel Kahneman* in 2002.

Summary

Eyewitness Testimony is a foundational text in the field of psychology. Those who want to study memory should certainly read it, as it offers a cohesive review of the relevant research on the human memory system. That it applies these ideas to the criminal justice system only makes the book more generally appealing, as it shows how psychology can inform the law.

This book would certainly have been less successful if it had not been so accessible. Its arguments are logical, and it clearly lays out the implications of those arguments for the criminal justice system. This is perhaps why it has the rare distinction among academic texts of profoundly influencing a social institution (in this case, the criminal justice system).

Eyewitness Testimony is a significant reason why Elizabeth F. Loftus is considered one of the most important figures in the history of modern psychology. In fact, she has been ranked as the most influential female psychologist in history.[2] Serious students of psychology or law can be expected to find the work a valuable resource.

NOTES

1   Moheb Costandi, "Evidence-Based Justice: Corrupted Memory," *Nature* 500, no. 7462 (August 2013): 269–70, http://dx.doi.org/10.1038/500268a, accessed February 16, 2016.

2   Steven J. Haggbloom et al., "The 100 Most Eminent Psychologists of the 20th Century," *Review of General Psychology* 6, no. 2 (2002): 139–52.

GLOSSARY OF TERMS

Acquisition: the stage of the human memory system at which people take in information.

Anthropology: the study of humankind, commonly conducted through research into societies, cultures, beliefs, and so on.

American Psychological Association (APA): the foremost professional organization for those who study psychology.

Applied research: the use of academic research to explain or better understand how something works in a nonacademic setting.

Behaviorist: an influential perspective in psychology based on the belief that we can understand people by observing how they act, and that we cannot study phenomena that we cannot observe.

Cognitive revolution: an intellectual movement of the 1950s that helped to establish the discipline of cognitive science.

Cognitive science: the scientific study of how the mind works.

Criminal justice system: the system of organizations, including the police and law courts, that work together to enforce laws and prosecute those who break them.

Empiricism: the belief that the world can only be known through observation. Empirical research methods rely on gathering data through what the researcher notices with his or her senses.

Eyewitness testimony: an account of an event given by the one who claims to have observed it.

Fallible: capable of making mistakes.

False memories: apparent recollections of events that did not actually occur.

Forgetting curve: a term coined by the German psychologist Hermann Ebbinghaus that describes how we forget a great deal immediately after witnessing an event, but as more and more time passes, the amount we forget about the event actually decreases.

Forensic science: the use of scientific methods and knowledge to solve crimes.

Linguistics: the study of the nature and structures of language.

Linguistic framing: the idea that the way a question is worded can affect how it is answered.

Malleable: capable of being shaped or changed.

Memory wars: the controversy in the 1990s between healthcare professionals about the reliability of repressed memories.

Neuroscience: scientific inquiry into the functioning of the human brain and nervous system.

Psychology: the scientific study of the mind and behavior.

Psychology and law: an area of academic study that focuses on how psychological principles can be used to inform legal proceedings.

Repressed memories: unconscious memories of traumatic events.

Retention: the stage of the human memory system at which information is stored.

Retrieval: the stage of the human memory system at which information is recalled.

Semantic memory: the type of memory that stores general knowledge.

Semantic retrieval: the ability to recall the general knowledge stored in semantic memory.

Sodium amytal: a barbiturate drug colloquially known as a "truth serum" when administered intravenously. This practice is highly controversial because the drug can induce a hypnotic-like state in which the individual may be more susceptible to the power of suggestion.

Theoretical research: research that contributes to a conceptual understanding of its subject.

Verbal overshadowing: the idea that when a witness describes a memory, the description can reshape that memory.

PEOPLE MENTIONED IN THE TEXT

Hermann Ebbinghaus (1850–1909) was a German psychologist who studied memory. Ebbinghaus is best known for his description of the forgetting curve.

Jonathan Freedman (b. 1937) is an American psychologist best known for postulating the foot-in-the-door phenomenon (the idea that is possible to get someone to agree to a major request by first getting them to agree to a smaller one). Dr. Freedman collaborated with Elizabeth Loftus during her graduate career at Stanford.

Daniel Kahneman (b. 1934) is an Israeli American psychologist and economist. Dr. Kahneman is best known for his work in behavioral economics and won the Nobel Prize in economics in 2002.

John Monahan (b. 1946) is an American psychologist and legal scholar. He holds the John S. Shannon Professorship of Law at the University of Virginia School of Law.

Allan Paivio (b. 1925) is a Canadian psychologist best known for his work on how verbal and nonverbal information are stored in memory. Dr. Paivio is an emeritus professor of psychology at the University of Western Ontario.

David Rumelhart (1942–2011) was an American psychologist; he is best known for his work on human cognition and cognitive neuroscience.

Jonathan Schooler (b. 1959) is an American psychologist best known for his work in cognitive psychology. Dr. Schooler is a professor of cognitive and social psychology at the University of California, Santa Barbara.

Edward E. Smith (1940–2012) was an American psychologist who specialized in cognitive science.

Patrick Suppes (1922–2014) was an American philosopher and scientist who was very concerned with cognitive science and educational technology. Dr. Suppes was also Elizabeth Loftus's mentor in graduate school.

Endel Tulving (b. 1927) is an Estonian Canadian psychologist best known for his work on the human memory system. Dr. Tulving is an emeritus professor of psychology at the University of Toronto.

Amos Tversky (1937–96) was an Israeli psychologist. Tversky collaborated with Daniel Kahneman in the work that led to Kahneman's Nobel Prize in economics in 2002.

Bessel van der Kolk (b. 1943) is a Dutch psychiatrist best known for his research on post-traumatic stress. Dr. van der Kolk is professor of psychiatry at Boston University.

WORKS CITED

WORKS CITED

American Psychological Association. "American Psychology-Law Society." Accessed December 8, 2015. http://www.apa.org/about/division/div41.aspx.

Batchelder, William H. and Kenneth Wexler. "Suppes' Work in the Foundations of Psychology." In *Patrick Suppes,* edited by Radu J. Bogdan, 149–86. Dordrecht, Holland: Springer, 1979.

Bourne, Lyle E., Roger L. Dominowski, and Elizabeth F. Loftus. *Cognitive Processes*. Englewood Cliffs, New Jersey: Prentice-Hall, 1979.

Bower, Gordon H. "Tracking the Birth of a Star." In *Do Justice and Let the Sky Fall: Elizabeth F. Loftus and Her Contributions to Science, Law, and Academic Freedom*, edited by Maryanne Garry and Harlene Hayne, 15–26. Mahwah, New Jersey: Lawrence Erlbaum Associates, 2007.

Brigham, John C. and Robert K. Bothwell. "The Ability of Prospective Jurors to Estimate the Accuracy of Eyewitness Identifications." *Law and Human Behavior* 7, no. 1 (1983): 19–30.

Chin, Jason M. and Jonathan W. Schooler. "Verbal Overshadowing and Eyewitness Identification." In *Encyclopedia of Psychology and Law,* edited by Brian L. Cutler, 831–3. Thousand Oaks, California: Sage, 2007.

Costandi, Moheb. "Evidence-Based Justice: Corrupted Memory." *Nature* 500, no. 7462 (August 2013): 268–70. Accessed February 16, 2016. http://dx.doi.org/10.1038/500268a.

Cutler, Brian L., Steven D. Penrod, and Hedy Red Dexter. "Juror Sensitivity to Eyewitness Identification Evidence." *Law and Human Behavior* 14, no. 2 (1990): 185–91.

Cutler, Brian L., Steven D. Penrod, and Thomas E. Stuve. "Juror Decision Making in Eyewitness Identification Cases." *Law and Human Behavior* 12, no. 1 (1988): 41–55.

Famous Psychologists. "Elizabeth Loftus." Accessed December 1, 2015. http://www.famouspsychologists.org/elizabeth-loftus/.

Findlaw. "State v. Henderson." Supreme Court of New Jersey (August 24, 2011). Accessed February 16, 2016. http://caselaw.findlaw.com/nj-supreme-court/1578475.html.

Friedman, Michael. "Patrick Suppes, Stanford Philosopher, Scientist, and Silicone Valley Entrepreneur, Dies at 92." *Stanford News* (November 25, 2014). Accessed December 1, 2015. http://news.stanford.edu/news/2014/november/patrick-suppes-obit-112514.

Garry, Maryanne and Hayne, Harlene, editors. *Do Justice and Let the Sky Fall: Elizabeth F. Loftus and Her Contributions to Science, Law, and Academic Freedom*. Mahwah, New Jersey: Lawrence Erlbaum Associates, 2007.

Geis, Gilbert and Elizabeth F. Loftus. "Taus vs. Loftus: Determining the Legal Ground Rules for Scholarly Inquiry." *Journal of Forensic Psychology Practice* 9 (2009): 147–62. Accessed February 16, 2016. http://papers.ssrn.com/sol3/papers.cfm?abstract_id=1496006.

Haggbloom, Steven J., Renee Warnick, Jason E. Warnick, Vinessa K. Jones, Gary L. Yarbrough, Tenea M. Russell, Chris M. Borecky, Reagan McGahhey, John L. Powell III, Jamie Beavers, and Emmanuelle Monte. "The 100 Most Eminent Psychologists of the 20th Century." *Review of General Psychology* 6, no. 2 (2002): 139–52.

Loftus, Elizabeth F. "Dispatch from the (Un)civil Memory Wars." *Lancet* 364 (December 2004): 20–1. Accessed February 16, 2016.

http://dx.doi.org/10.1016/S0140-6736(04)17626-5.

_____. *Eyewitness Testimony*. Cambridge, MA: Harvard University Press, 1996.

Loftus, Elizabeth F. and Deborah Davis. "Recovered Memories." *Annual Review of Clinical Psychology* 2 (April 2006): 469–98.

Loftus, Elizabeth F. and Melvin J. Guyer. "Who Abused Jane Doe? The Hazards of the Single Case History: Part I." *Skeptical Inquirer* 26, no. 3 (2002): 24–32.

Loftus, Elizabeth F. and Jacqueline E. Pickrell. "The Formation of False Memories." *Psychiatric Annals* 25, no. 12 (December 1995): 720–5.

Loftus, Geoffrey R. and Elizabeth F. Loftus. *Human Memory: The Processing of Information*. Hillsdale, New Jersey: Lawrence Erlbaum Associates, 1976.

Mednick, Sarnoff A., Howard R. Pollio, and Elizabeth F. Loftus. *Learning*. Englewood Cliffs, New Jersey: Prentice-Hall, 1973.

Miller, George A. "The Cognitive Revolution: A Historical Perspective." *Trends in Cognitive Sciences* 7, no. 3 (March 2003): 141–4.

Monahan, John and Elizabeth F. Loftus. "The Psychology of Law." *Annual Review of Psychology* 33 (February 1982): 441–75. Accessed February 16, 2016. http://dx.doi.org/10.1146/annurev.ps.33.020182.002301.

Neimark, Jill. "The Diva of Disclosure, Memory Researcher Elizabeth Loftus." *Psychology Today* 29, no. 1 (January 1996): 48.

Pachella, Robert G. "Personal Values and the Value of Expert Testimony." *Law and Human Behavior* 10, no. 1–2 (June 1986): 145–50.

Patihis, Lawrence, Lavina Y. Ho, Ian W. Tingen, Scott O. Lilienfeld, and Elizabeth F. Loftus. "Are the 'Memory Wars' Over? A Scientist-Practitioner Gap in Beliefs about Repressed Memory." *Psychological Science* 25, no. 2 (February 2014): 519–30.

Schooler, Jonathan W. and Tonya Y. Engstler-Schooler. "Verbal Overshadowing of Visual Memories: Some Things are Better Left Unsaid." *Cognitive Psychology* 22 (1990): 36–71.

Schooler, Jonathan W., Robert S. Ryan, and Lynne Reder. "The Costs and Benefits of Verbally Rehearsing Memory for Faces." In *Basic and Applied Memory Research, Volume II,* edited by D. J. Herrmann, M. K. Johnson, C. Hertzog, C. McEvoy, and P. Hertel, 51–65. Hillsdale, New Jersey: Lawrence Erlbaum Associates, 1996.

Shaw, Julia. "Memory Mondays: 'Regression Therapy' isn't Real, but Hollywood Keeps the Myth Alive." *Scientific American* (November 23, 2015). Accessed December 9, 2015. http://blogs.scientificamerican.com/mind-guest-blog/memory-mondays-regression-therapy-isn-t-real-but-hollywood-keeps-the-myth-alive/.

Simon, Jonathan. *Governing through Crime: How the War on Crime Transformed American Democracy and Created a Culture of Fear.* Oxford: Oxford University Press, 2007.

University of California Irvine School of Social Ecology. "Elizabeth F. Loftus: Curriculum Vitae." Accessed December 1, 2015. http://socialecology.uci.edu/faculty/eloftus.

van der Kolk, Bessel A. and Rita Fisler. "Dissociation and the Fragmentary Nature of Traumatic Memories: Overview and Exploratory Study." *Journal of Traumatic Stress* 8, no. 4 (1995): 505–25.

THE MACAT LIBRARY
BY DISCIPLINE

The Macat Library By Discipline

AFRICANA STUDIES

Chinua Achebe's *An Image of Africa: Racism in Conrad's Heart of Darkness*
W. E. B. Du Bois's *The Souls of Black Folk*
Zora Neale Huston's *Characteristics of Negro Expression*
Martin Luther King Jr's *Why We Can't Wait*
Toni Morrison's *Playing in the Dark: Whiteness in the American Literary Imagination*

ANTHROPOLOGY

Arjun Appadurai's *Modernity at Large: Cultural Dimensions of Globalisation*
Philippe Ariès's *Centuries of Childhood*
Franz Boas's *Race, Language and Culture*
Kim Chan & Renée Mauborgne's *Blue Ocean Strategy*
Jared Diamond's *Guns, Germs & Steel: the Fate of Human Societies*
Jared Diamond's *Collapse: How Societies Choose to Fail or Survive*
E. E. Evans-Pritchard's *Witchcraft, Oracles and Magic Among the Azande*
James Ferguson's *The Anti-Politics Machine*
Clifford Geertz's *The Interpretation of Cultures*
David Graeber's *Debt: the First 5000 Years*
Karen Ho's *Liquidated: An Ethnography of Wall Street*
Geert Hofstede's *Culture's Consequences: Comparing Values, Behaviors, Institutes and Organizations across Nations*
Claude Lévi-Strauss's *Structural Anthropology*
Jay Macleod's *Ain't No Makin' It: Aspirations and Attainment in a Low-Income Neighborhood*
Saba Mahmood's *The Politics of Piety: The Islamic Revival and the Feminist Subject*
Marcel Mauss's *The Gift*

BUSINESS

Jean Lave & Etienne Wenger's *Situated Learning*
Theodore Levitt's *Marketing Myopia*
Burton G. Malkiel's *A Random Walk Down Wall Street*
Douglas McGregor's *The Human Side of Enterprise*
Michael Porter's *Competitive Strategy: Creating and Sustaining Superior Performance*
John Kotter's *Leading Change*
C. K. Prahalad & Gary Hamel's *The Core Competence of the Corporation*

CRIMINOLOGY

Michelle Alexander's *The New Jim Crow: Mass Incarceration in the Age of Colorblindness*
Michael R. Gottfredson & Travis Hirschi's *A General Theory of Crime*
Richard Herrnstein & Charles A. Murray's *The Bell Curve: Intelligence and Class Structure in American Life*
Elizabeth Loftus's *Eyewitness Testimony*
Jay Macleod's *Ain't No Makin' It: Aspirations and Attainment in a Low-Income Neighborhood*
Philip Zimbardo's *The Lucifer Effect*

ECONOMICS

Janet Abu-Lughod's *Before European Hegemony*
Ha-Joon Chang's *Kicking Away the Ladder*
David Brion Davis's *The Problem of Slavery in the Age of Revolution*
Milton Friedman's *The Role of Monetary Policy*
Milton Friedman's *Capitalism and Freedom*
David Graeber's *Debt: the First 5000 Years*
Friedrich Hayek's *The Road to Serfdom*
Karen Ho's *Liquidated: An Ethnography of Wall Street*

John Maynard Keynes's *The General Theory of Employment, Interest and Money*
Charles P. Kindleberger's *Manias, Panics and Crashes*
Robert Lucas's *Why Doesn't Capital Flow from Rich to Poor Countries?*
Burton G. Malkiel's *A Random Walk Down Wall Street*
Thomas Robert Malthus's *An Essay on the Principle of Population*
Karl Marx's *Capital*
Thomas Piketty's *Capital in the Twenty-First Century*
Amartya Sen's *Development as Freedom*
Adam Smith's *The Wealth of Nations*
Nassim Nicholas Taleb's *The Black Swan: The Impact of the Highly Improbable*
Amos Tversky's & Daniel Kahneman's *Judgment under Uncertainty: Heuristics and Biases*
Mahbub Ul Haq's *Reflections on Human Development*
Max Weber's *The Protestant Ethic and the Spirit of Capitalism*

FEMINISM AND GENDER STUDIES

Judith Butler's *Gender Trouble*
Simone De Beauvoir's *The Second Sex*
Michel Foucault's *History of Sexuality*
Betty Friedan's *The Feminine Mystique*
Saba Mahmood's *The Politics of Piety: The Islamic Revival and the Feminist Subject*
Joan Wallach Scott's *Gender and the Politics of History*
Mary Wollstonecraft's *A Vindication of the Rights of Woman*
Virginia Woolf's *A Room of One's Own*

GEOGRAPHY

The Brundtland Report's *Our Common Future*
Rachel Carson's *Silent Spring*
Charles Darwin's *On the Origin of Species*
James Ferguson's *The Anti-Politics Machine*
Jane Jacobs's *The Death and Life of Great American Cities*
James Lovelock's *Gaia: A New Look at Life on Earth*
Amartya Sen's *Development as Freedom*
Mathis Wackernagel & William Rees's *Our Ecological Footprint*

HISTORY

Janet Abu-Lughod's *Before European Hegemony*
Benedict Anderson's *Imagined Communities*
Bernard Bailyn's *The Ideological Origins of the American Revolution*
Hanna Batatu's *The Old Social Classes And The Revolutionary Movements Of Iraq*
Christopher Browning's *Ordinary Men: Reserve Police Batallion 101 and the Final Solution in Poland*
Edmund Burke's *Reflections on the Revolution in France*
William Cronon's *Nature's Metropolis: Chicago And The Great West*
Alfred W. Crosby's *The Columbian Exchange*
Hamid Dabashi's *Iran: A People Interrupted*
David Brion Davis's *The Problem of Slavery in the Age of Revolution*
Nathalie Zemon Davis's *The Return of Martin Guerre*
Jared Diamond's *Guns, Germs & Steel: the Fate of Human Societies*
Frank Dikotter's *Mao's Great Famine*
John W Dower's *War Without Mercy: Race And Power In The Pacific War*
W. E. B. Du Bois's *The Souls of Black Folk*
Richard J. Evans's *In Defence of History*
Lucien Febvre's *The Problem of Unbelief in the 16th Century*
Sheila Fitzpatrick's *Everyday Stalinism*

The Macat Library By Discipline

Eric Foner's *Reconstruction: America's Unfinished Revolution, 1863-1877*
Michel Foucault's *Discipline and Punish*
Michel Foucault's *History of Sexuality*
Francis Fukuyama's *The End of History and the Last Man*
John Lewis Gaddis's *We Now Know: Rethinking Cold War History*
Ernest Gellner's *Nations and Nationalism*
Eugene Genovese's *Roll, Jordan, Roll: The World the Slaves Made*
Carlo Ginzburg's *The Night Battles*
Daniel Goldhagen's *Hitler's Willing Executioners*
Jack Goldstone's *Revolution and Rebellion in the Early Modern World*
Antonio Gramsci's *The Prison Notebooks*
Alexander Hamilton, John Jay & James Madison's *The Federalist Papers*
Christopher Hill's *The World Turned Upside Down*
Carole Hillenbrand's *The Crusades: Islamic Perspectives*
Thomas Hobbes's *Leviathan*
Eric Hobsbawm's *The Age Of Revolution*
John A. Hobson's *Imperialism: A Study*
Albert Hourani's *History of the Arab Peoples*
Samuel P. Huntington's *The Clash of Civilizations and the Remaking of World Order*
C. L. R. James's *The Black Jacobins*
Tony Judt's *Postwar: A History of Europe Since 1945*
Ernst Kantorowicz's *The King's Two Bodies: A Study in Medieval Political Theology*
Paul Kennedy's *The Rise and Fall of the Great Powers*
Ian Kershaw's *The "Hitler Myth": Image and Reality in the Third Reich*
John Maynard Keynes's *The General Theory of Employment, Interest and Money*
Charles P. Kindleberger's *Manias, Panics and Crashes*
Martin Luther King Jr's *Why We Can't Wait*
Henry Kissinger's *World Order: Reflections on the Character of Nations and the Course of History*
Thomas Kuhn's *The Structure of Scientific Revolutions*
Georges Lefebvre's *The Coming of the French Revolution*
John Locke's *Two Treatises of Government*
Niccolò Machiavelli's *The Prince*
Thomas Robert Malthus's *An Essay on the Principle of Population*
Mahmood Mamdani's *Citizen and Subject: Contemporary Africa And The Legacy Of Late Colonialism*
Karl Marx's *Capital*
Stanley Milgram's *Obedience to Authority*
John Stuart Mill's *On Liberty*
Thomas Paine's *Common Sense*
Thomas Paine's *Rights of Man*
Geoffrey Parker's *Global Crisis: War, Climate Change and Catastrophe in the Seventeenth Century*
Jonathan Riley-Smith's *The First Crusade and the Idea of Crusading*
Jean-Jacques Rousseau's *The Social Contract*
Joan Wallach Scott's *Gender and the Politics of History*
Theda Skocpol's *States and Social Revolutions*
Adam Smith's *The Wealth of Nations*
Timothy Snyder's *Bloodlands: Europe Between Hitler and Stalin*
Sun Tzu's *The Art of War*
Keith Thomas's *Religion and the Decline of Magic*
Thucydides's *The History of the Peloponnesian War*
Frederick Jackson Turner's *The Significance of the Frontier in American History*
Odd Arne Westad's *The Global Cold War: Third World Interventions And The Making Of Our Times*

LITERATURE

Chinua Achebe's *An Image of Africa: Racism in Conrad's Heart of Darkness*
Roland Barthes's *Mythologies*
Homi K. Bhabha's *The Location of Culture*
Judith Butler's *Gender Trouble*
Simone De Beauvoir's *The Second Sex*
Ferdinand De Saussure's *Course in General Linguistics*
T. S. Eliot's *The Sacred Wood: Essays on Poetry and Criticism*
Zora Neale Huston's *Characteristics of Negro Expression*
Toni Morrison's *Playing in the Dark: Whiteness in the American Literary Imagination*
Edward Said's *Orientalism*
Gayatri Chakravorty Spivak's *Can the Subaltern Speak?*
Mary Wollstonecraft's *A Vindication of the Rights of Women*
Virginia Woolf's *A Room of One's Own*

PHILOSOPHY

Elizabeth Anscombe's *Modern Moral Philosophy*
Hannah Arendt's *The Human Condition*
Aristotle's *Metaphysics*
Aristotle's *Nicomachean Ethics*
Edmund Gettier's *Is Justified True Belief Knowledge?*
Georg Wilhelm Friedrich Hegel's *Phenomenology of Spirit*
David Hume's *Dialogues Concerning Natural Religion*
David Hume's *The Enquiry for Human Understanding*
Immanuel Kant's *Religion within the Boundaries of Mere Reason*
Immanuel Kant's *Critique of Pure Reason*
Søren Kierkegaard's *The Sickness Unto Death*
Søren Kierkegaard's *Fear and Trembling*
C. S. Lewis's *The Abolition of Man*
Alasdair MacIntyre's *After Virtue*
Marcus Aurelius's *Meditations*
Friedrich Nietzsche's *On the Genealogy of Morality*
Friedrich Nietzsche's *Beyond Good and Evil*
Plato's *Republic*
Plato's *Symposium*
Jean-Jacques Rousseau's *The Social Contract*
Gilbert Ryle's *The Concept of Mind*
Baruch Spinoza's *Ethics*
Sun Tzu's *The Art of War*
Ludwig Wittgenstein's *Philosophical Investigations*

POLITICS

Benedict Anderson's *Imagined Communities*
Aristotle's *Politics*
Bernard Bailyn's *The Ideological Origins of the American Revolution*
Edmund Burke's *Reflections on the Revolution in France*
John C. Calhoun's *A Disquisition on Government*
Ha-Joon Chang's *Kicking Away the Ladder*
Hamid Dabashi's *Iran: A People Interrupted*
Hamid Dabashi's *Theology of Discontent: The Ideological Foundation of the Islamic Revolution in Iran*
Robert Dahl's *Democracy and its Critics*
Robert Dahl's *Who Governs?*
David Brion Davis's *The Problem of Slavery in the Age of Revolution*

The Macat Library By Discipline

Alexis De Tocqueville's *Democracy in America*
James Ferguson's *The Anti-Politics Machine*
Frank Dikotter's *Mao's Great Famine*
Sheila Fitzpatrick's *Everyday Stalinism*
Eric Foner's *Reconstruction: America's Unfinished Revolution, 1863-1877*
Milton Friedman's *Capitalism and Freedom*
Francis Fukuyama's *The End of History and the Last Man*
John Lewis Gaddis's *We Now Know: Rethinking Cold War History*
Ernest Gellner's *Nations and Nationalism*
David Graeber's *Debt: the First 5000 Years*
Antonio Gramsci's *The Prison Notebooks*
Alexander Hamilton, John Jay & James Madison's *The Federalist Papers*
Friedrich Hayek's *The Road to Serfdom*
Christopher Hill's *The World Turned Upside Down*
Thomas Hobbes's *Leviathan*
John A. Hobson's *Imperialism: A Study*
Samuel P. Huntington's *The Clash of Civilizations and the Remaking of World Order*
Tony Judt's *Postwar: A History of Europe Since 1945*
David C. Kang's *China Rising: Peace, Power and Order in East Asia*
Paul Kennedy's *The Rise and Fall of Great Powers*
Robert Keohane's *After Hegemony*
Martin Luther King Jr.'s *Why We Can't Wait*
Henry Kissinger's *World Order: Reflections on the Character of Nations and the Course of History*
John Locke's *Two Treatises of Government*
Niccolò Machiavelli's *The Prince*
Thomas Robert Malthus's *An Essay on the Principle of Population*
Mahmood Mamdani's *Citizen and Subject: Contemporary Africa And The Legacy Of Late Colonialism*
Karl Marx's *Capital*
John Stuart Mill's *On Liberty*
John Stuart Mill's *Utilitarianism*
Hans Morgenthau's *Politics Among Nations*
Thomas Paine's *Common Sense*
Thomas Paine's *Rights of Man*
Thomas Piketty's *Capital in the Twenty-First Century*
Robert D. Putman's *Bowling Alone*
John Rawls's *Theory of Justice*
Jean-Jacques Rousseau's *The Social Contract*
Theda Skocpol's *States and Social Revolutions*
Adam Smith's *The Wealth of Nations*
Sun Tzu's *The Art of War*
Henry David Thoreau's *Civil Disobedience*
Thucydides's *The History of the Peloponnesian War*
Kenneth Waltz's *Theory of International Politics*
Max Weber's *Politics as a Vocation*
Odd Arne Westad's *The Global Cold War: Third World Interventions And The Making Of Our Times*

POSTCOLONIAL STUDIES

Roland Barthes's *Mythologies*
Frantz Fanon's *Black Skin, White Masks*
Homi K. Bhabha's *The Location of Culture*
Gustavo Gutiérrez's *A Theology of Liberation*
Edward Said's *Orientalism*
Gayatri Chakravorty Spivak's *Can the Subaltern Speak?*

PSYCHOLOGY

Gordon Allport's *The Nature of Prejudice*
Alan Baddeley & Graham Hitch's *Aggression: A Social Learning Analysis*
Albert Bandura's *Aggression: A Social Learning Analysis*
Leon Festinger's *A Theory of Cognitive Dissonance*
Sigmund Freud's *The Interpretation of Dreams*
Betty Friedan's *The Feminine Mystique*
Michael R. Gottfredson & Travis Hirschi's *A General Theory of Crime*
Eric Hoffer's *The True Believer: Thoughts on the Nature of Mass Movements*
William James's *Principles of Psychology*
Elizabeth Loftus's *Eyewitness Testimony*
A. H. Maslow's *A Theory of Human Motivation*
Stanley Milgram's *Obedience to Authority*
Steven Pinker's *The Better Angels of Our Nature*
Oliver Sacks's *The Man Who Mistook His Wife For a Hat*
Richard Thaler & Cass Sunstein's *Nudge: Improving Decisions About Health, Wealth and Happiness*
Amos Tversky's *Judgment under Uncertainty: Heuristics and Biases*
Philip Zimbardo's *The Lucifer Effect*

SCIENCE

Rachel Carson's *Silent Spring*
William Cronon's *Nature's Metropolis: Chicago And The Great West*
Alfred W. Crosby's *The Columbian Exchange*
Charles Darwin's *On the Origin of Species*
Richard Dawkin's *The Selfish Gene*
Thomas Kuhn's *The Structure of Scientific Revolutions*
Geoffrey Parker's *Global Crisis: War, Climate Change and Catastrophe in the Seventeenth Century*
Mathis Wackernagel & William Rees's *Our Ecological Footprint*

SOCIOLOGY

Michelle Alexander's *The New Jim Crow: Mass Incarceration in the Age of Colorblindness*
Gordon Allport's *The Nature of Prejudice*
Albert Bandura's *Aggression: A Social Learning Analysis*
Hanna Batatu's *The Old Social Classes And The Revolutionary Movements Of Iraq*
Ha-Joon Chang's *Kicking Away the Ladder*
W. E. B. Du Bois's *The Souls of Black Folk*
Émile Durkheim's *On Suicide*
Frantz Fanon's *Black Skin, White Masks*
Frantz Fanon's *The Wretched of the Earth*
Eric Foner's *Reconstruction: America's Unfinished Revolution, 1863-1877*
Eugene Genovese's *Roll, Jordan, Roll: The World the Slaves Made*
Jack Goldstone's *Revolution and Rebellion in the Early Modern World*
Antonio Gramsci's *The Prison Notebooks*
Richard Herrnstein & Charles A Murray's *The Bell Curve: Intelligence and Class Structure in American Life*
Eric Hoffer's *The True Believer: Thoughts on the Nature of Mass Movements*
Jane Jacobs's *The Death and Life of Great American Cities*
Robert Lucas's *Why Doesn't Capital Flow from Rich to Poor Countries?*
Jay Macleod's *Ain't No Makin' It: Aspirations and Attainment in a Low Income Neighborhood*
Elaine May's *Homeward Bound: American Families in the Cold War Era*
Douglas McGregor's *The Human Side of Enterprise*
C. Wright Mills's *The Sociological Imagination*

The Macat Library By Discipline

Thomas Piketty's *Capital in the Twenty-First Century*
Robert D. Putman's *Bowling Alone*
David Riesman's *The Lonely Crowd: A Study of the Changing American Character*
Edward Said's *Orientalism*
Joan Wallach Scott's *Gender and the Politics of History*
Theda Skocpol's *States and Social Revolutions*
Max Weber's *The Protestant Ethic and the Spirit of Capitalism*

THEOLOGY

Augustine's *Confessions*
Benedict's *Rule of St Benedict*
Gustavo Gutiérrez's *A Theology of Liberation*
Carole Hillenbrand's *The Crusades: Islamic Perspectives*
David Hume's *Dialogues Concerning Natural Religion*
Immanuel Kant's *Religion within the Boundaries of Mere Reason*
Ernst Kantorowicz's *The King's Two Bodies: A Study in Medieval Political Theology*
Søren Kierkegaard's *The Sickness Unto Death*
C. S. Lewis's *The Abolition of Man*
Saba Mahmood's *The Politics of Piety: The Islamic Revival and the Feminist Subject*
Baruch Spinoza's *Ethics*
Keith Thomas's *Religion and the Decline of Magic*

COMING SOON

Chris Argyris's *The Individual and the Organisation*
Seyla Benhabib's *The Rights of Others*
Walter Benjamin's *The Work Of Art in the Age of Mechanical Reproduction*
John Berger's *Ways of Seeing*
Pierre Bourdieu's *Outline of a Theory of Practice*
Mary Douglas's *Purity and Danger*
Roland Dworkin's *Taking Rights Seriously*
James G. March's *Exploration and Exploitation in Organisational Learning*
Ikujiro Nonaka's *A Dynamic Theory of Organizational Knowledge Creation*
Griselda Pollock's *Vision and Difference*
Amartya Sen's *Inequality Re-Examined*
Susan Sontag's *On Photography*
Yasser Tabbaa's *The Transformation of Islamic Art*
Ludwig von Mises's *Theory of Money and Credit*

Macat Disciplines

Access the greatest ideas and thinkers across entire disciplines, including

Postcolonial Studies

Roland Barthes's *Mythologies*
Frantz Fanon's *Black Skin, White Masks*
Homi K. Bhabha's *The Location of Culture*
Gustavo Gutiérrez's *A Theology of Liberation*
Edward Said's *Orientalism*
Gayatri Chakravorty Spivak's *Can the Subaltern Speak?*

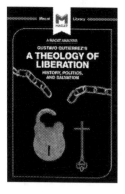
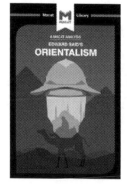

Macat analyses are available from all good bookshops and libraries.

Access hundreds of analyses through one, multimedia tool.

Join free for one month **library.macat.com**

Macat Disciplines

Access the greatest ideas and thinkers across entire disciplines, including

AFRICANA STUDIES

Chinua Achebe's *An Image of Africa: Racism in Conrad's Heart of Darkness*

W. E. B. Du Bois's *The Souls of Black Folk*

Zora Neale Hurston's *Characteristics of Negro Expression*

Martin Luther King Jr.'s *Why We Can't Wait*

Toni Morrison's *Playing in the Dark: Whiteness in the American Literary Imagination*

Macat analyses are available from all good bookshops and libraries.

Access hundreds of analyses through one, multimedia tool.

Join free for one month **library.macat.com**

Macat Disciplines

Access the greatest ideas and thinkers across entire disciplines, including

FEMINISM, GENDER AND QUEER STUDIES

Simone De Beauvoir's
The Second Sex

Michel Foucault's
History of Sexuality

Betty Friedan's
The Feminine Mystique

Saba Mahmood's
*The Politics of Piety:
The Islamic Revival and
the Feminist Subject*

Joan Wallach Scott's
*Gender and the
Politics of History*

Mary Wollstonecraft's
*A Vindication of the
Rights of Woman*

Virginia Woolf's
A Room of One's Own

Judith Butler's
Gender Trouble

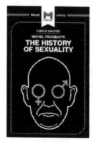

Macat analyses are available from all good bookshops and libraries.

Access hundreds of analyses through one, multimedia tool.

Join free for one month library.macat.com

Macat Disciplines

Access the greatest ideas and thinkers across entire disciplines, including

INEQUALITY

Ha-Joon Chang's, *Kicking Away the Ladder*
David Graeber's, *Debt: The First 5000 Years*
Robert E. Lucas's, *Why Doesn't Capital Flow from Rich To Poor Countries?*
Thomas Piketty's, *Capital in the Twenty-First Century*
Amartya Sen's, *Inequality Re-Examined*
Mahbub Ul Haq's, *Reflections on Human Development*

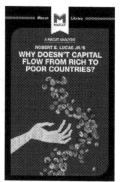

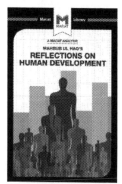

Macat analyses are available from all good bookshops and libraries.

Access hundreds of analyses through one, multimedia tool.

Join free for one month **library.macat.com**

Macat Disciplines

Access the greatest ideas and thinkers across entire disciplines, including

GLOBALIZATION

Arjun Appadurai's, *Modernity at Large: Cultural Dimensions of Globalisation*

James Ferguson's, *The Anti-Politics Machine*

Geert Hofstede's, *Culture's Consequences*

Amartya Sen's, *Development as Freedom*

Macat analyses are available from all good bookshops and libraries.

Access hundreds of analyses through one, multimedia tool.

Join free for one month **library.macat.com**

Macat Disciplines

Access the greatest ideas and thinkers across entire disciplines, including

MAN AND THE ENVIRONMENT

The Brundtland Report's, *Our Common Future*

Rachel Carson's, *Silent Spring*

James Lovelock's, *Gaia: A New Look at Life on Earth*

Mathis Wackernagel & William Rees's, *Our Ecological Footprint*

Macat analyses are available from all good bookshops and libraries.

Access hundreds of analyses through one, multimedia tool.
Join free for one month **library.macat.com**

Macat Disciplines

Access the greatest ideas and thinkers across entire disciplines, including

TOTALITARIANISM

Sheila Fitzpatrick's, *Everyday Stalinism*
Ian Kershaw's, *The "Hitler Myth"*
Timothy Snyder's, *Bloodlands*

Macat Pairs

Analyse historical and modern issues from opposite sides of an argument. Pairs include:

RACE AND IDENTITY

Zora Neale Hurston's
Characteristics of Negro Expression

Using material collected on anthropological expeditions to the South, Zora Neale Hurston explains how expression in African American culture in the early twentieth century departs from the art of white America. At the time, African American art was often criticized for copying white culture. For Hurston, this criticism misunderstood how art works. European tradition views art as something fixed. But Hurston describes a creative process that is alive, ever-changing, and largely improvisational. She maintains that African American art works through a process called 'mimicry'—where an imitated object or verbal pattern, for example, is reshaped and altered until it becomes something new, novel—and worthy of attention.

Frantz Fanon's
Black Skin, White Masks

Black Skin, White Masks offers a radical analysis of the psychological effects of colonization on the colonized.

Fanon witnessed the effects of colonization first hand both in his birthplace, Martinique, and again later in life when he worked as a psychiatrist in another French colony, Algeria. His text is uncompromising in form and argument. He dissects the dehumanizing effects of colonialism, arguing that it destroys the native sense of identity, forcing people to adapt to an alien set of values—including a core belief that they are inferior. This results in deep psychological trauma.

Fanon's work played a pivotal role in the civil rights movements of the 1960s.

Macat analyses are available from all good bookshops and libraries.

Access hundreds of analyses through one, multimedia tool.
Join free for one month **library.macat.com**

Macat Pairs

Analyse historical and modern issues from opposite sides of an argument. Pairs include:

INTERNATIONAL RELATIONS IN THE 21ST CENTURY

Samuel P. Huntington's
The Clash of Civilisations

In his highly influential 1996 book, Huntington offers a vision of a post-Cold War world in which conflict takes place not between competing ideologies but between cultures. The worst clash, he argues, will be between the Islamic world and the West: the West's arrogance and belief that its culture is a "gift" to the world will come into conflict with Islam's obstinacy and concern that its culture is under attack from a morally decadent "other."

Clash inspired much debate between different political schools of thought. But its greatest impact came in helping define American foreign policy in the wake of the 2001 terrorist attacks in New York and Washington.

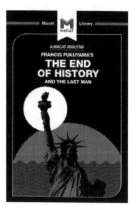

Francis Fukuyama's
The End of History and the Last Man

Published in 1992, *The End of History and the Last Man* argues that capitalist democracy is the final destination for all societies. Fukuyama believed democracy triumphed during the Cold War because it lacks the "fundamental contradictions" inherent in communism and satisfies our yearning for freedom and equality. Democracy therefore marks the endpoint in the evolution of ideology, and so the "end of history." There will still be "events," but no fundamental change in ideology.

Macat Pairs

Analyse historical and modern issues from opposite sides of an argument. Pairs include:

HOW TO RUN AN ECONOMY

John Maynard Keynes's
The General Theory OF Employment, Interest and Money

Classical economics suggests that market economies are self-correcting in times of recession or depression, and tend toward full employment and output. But English economist John Maynard Keynes disagrees.

In his ground-breaking 1936 study *The General Theory*, Keynes argues that traditional economics has misunderstood the causes of unemployment. Employment is not determined by the price of labor; it is directly linked to demand. Keynes believes market economies are by nature unstable, and so require government intervention. Spurred on by the social catastrophe of the Great Depression of the 1930s, he sets out to revolutionize the way the world thinks

Milton Friedman's
The Role of Monetary Policy

Friedman's 1968 paper changed the course of economic theory. In just 17 pages, he demolished existing theory and outlined an effective alternate monetary policy designed to secure 'high employment, stable prices and rapid growth.'

Friedman demonstrated that monetary policy plays a vital role in broader economic stability and argued that economists got their monetary policy wrong in the 1950s and 1960s by misunderstanding the relationship between inflation and unemployment. Previous generations of economists had believed that governments could permanently decrease unemployment by permitting inflation—and vice versa. Friedman's most original contribution was to show that this supposed trade-off is an illusion that only works in the short term.

Macat analyses are available from all good bookshops and libraries.

Access hundreds of analyses through one, multimedia tool.
Join free for one month **library.macat.com**

Macat Pairs

Analyse historical and modern issues
from opposite sides of an argument.
Pairs include:

ARE WE FUNDAMENTALLY GOOD - OR BAD?

Steven Pinker's
The Better Angels of Our Nature

Stephen Pinker's gloriously optimistic 2011 book argues that, despite humanity's biological tendency toward violence, we are, in fact, less violent today than ever before. To prove his case, Pinker lays out pages of detailed statistical evidence. For him, much of the credit for the decline goes to the eighteenth-century Enlightenment movement, whose ideas of liberty, tolerance, and respect for the value of human life filtered down through society and affected how people thought. That psychological change led to behavioral change—and overall we became more peaceful. Critics countered that humanity could never overcome the biological urge toward violence; others argued that Pinker's statistics were flawed.

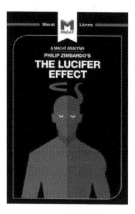

Philip Zimbardo's
The Lucifer Effect

Some psychologists believe those who commit cruelty are innately evil. Zimbardo disagrees. In *The Lucifer Effect*, he argues that sometimes good people do evil things simply because of the situations they find themselves in, citing many historical examples to illustrate his point. Zimbardo details his 1971 Stanford prison experiment, where ordinary volunteers playing guards in a mock prison rapidly became abusive. But he also describes the tortures committed by US army personnel in Iraq's Abu Ghraib prison in 2003—and how he himself testified in defence of one of those guards. committed by US army personnel in Iraq's Abu Ghraib prison in 2003—and how he himself testified in defence of one of those guards.

Macat analyses are available from all good bookshops and libraries.

Access hundreds of analyses through one, multimedia tool.

Join free for one month library

Macat Pairs

Analyse historical and modern issues from opposite sides of an argument. Pairs include:

Jean-Jacques Rousseau's
The Social Contract

Rousseau's famous work sets out the radical concept of the 'social contract': a give-and-take relationship between individual freedom and social order.

If people are free to do as they like, governed only by their own sense of justice, they are also vulnerable to chaos and violence. To avoid this, Rousseau proposes, they should agree to give up some freedom to benefit from the protection of social and political organization. But this deal is only just if societies are led by the collective needs and desires of the people, and able to control the private interests of individuals. For Rousseau, the only legitimate form of government is rule by the people.

Robert D. Putnam's
Bowling Alone

In *Bowling Alone*, Robert Putnam argues that Americans have become disconnected from one another and from the institutions of their common life, and investigates the consequences of this change.

Looking at a range of indicators, from membership in formal organizations to the number of invitations being extended to informal dinner parties, Putnam demonstrates that Americans are interacting less and creating less "social capital" – with potentially disastrous implications for their society.

It would be difficult to overstate the impact of *Bowling Alone*, one of the most frequently cited social science publications of the last half-century.